Experts and Environmental Planning

BOB EVANS

Avebury

Aldershot · Brookfield USA · Hong Kong · Singapore · Sydney

Published by
Avebury
Ashgate Publishing Limited
Gower House
Croft Road
Aldershot
Hants GU11 3HR
England

Ashgate Publishing Company
Old Post Road
Brookfield
Vermont 05036
USA

A CIP catalogue record for this book is available from the British Library.

Library of Congress Catalog Card Number: 94-74468

ISBN 1 85628 673 8

Printed and bound by Athenaeum Press Ltd.,
Gateshead, Tyne & Wear.

Contents

	List of tables	*vii*
Chapter One:	Introduction	1
Chapter Two:	The debate over the middle class	6
	The legacy of Marx and Weber	7
	The middle class as service class	10
	The class theories of E.O. Wright	17
	Bourdieu and cultural capital	18
	Assets and class formation	19
	Class analysis and the profession of town planning	24
Chapter Three:	Expert labour and power	28
	The nature of expert labour	29
	Professionalism and professionalisation	31
	Professionalisation and the state	35
	Professionalism and bureaucracy	37
	Expert labour and bureaucratic power	38
	Experts and state policy making	43
	Organisation assets, skill assets and expert labour	47
	Expert labour and town planning	49

Chapter Four:	The profession of planning	51
	The purpose of planning	52
	Planning, reform and the public interest	54
	The planning profession and internal conflict	60
	Planning and the process of professionalisation	64
	Professionalism and town planning	68
	Expertise and cognitive competence in planning	73
	Planning, professionalism and expertise	76
Chapter Five:	The planners	78
	The existing surveys	79
	The 1990 survey	88
	The questionnaire	90
	Personal characteristics of respondents	92
	Skill assets and credentials	96
	Economic assets	102
	Organisation assets	105
	Career, mobility and attachment to locality	111
	Views on the planning process	114
	Political attitudes	117
Chapter Six:	Conclusions	124
	Town planning and the 'corporatist bargain'	124
	Town planning, skills and expertise	129
	The 'asset approach' to class analysis	133
	Town planners, the middle class and the service class	137
	Town planning, politics and professionalism	141
Bibliography		143

List of tables

Table 5.1	Town planners: gender	93
Table 5.2	Town planners: self-assigned social class	94
Table 5.3	Class origin of town planners	95
Table 5.4	Membership of professional institutions	97
Table 5.5	Salaries and household income	103
Table 5.6	Percentage of respondents with another member of the household in paid employment	104
Table 5.7	Public sector planning experience of private sector respondents (percentage of respondents by most senior local government post held)	107
Table 5.8	Future mobility to the private sector by public sector planners	108-9
Table 5.9	Respondents' membership of local organisations	112
Table 5.10	Attachment of respondents to locality	112-13
Table 5.11	Professional responsibility	115
Table 5.12	Beneficiaries of the planning process	116
Table 5.13	Voting intentions	118
Table 5.14	Attitudinal questions - public sector respondents	120
Table 5.15	Attitudinal questions - private sector respondents	121

1 Introduction

It is now nearly one hundred years since Ebenezer Howard published *Tomorrow: A Peaceful Path to Land Reform*, later to be entitled *Garden Cities of Tomorrow* and arguably the most important and influential single text in the development of land use planning in Britain. This book was to lay the foundation stones for the garden city experiments and later the wider town planning movement which were together to mature into an important area of post-1945 government policy. Town planning was to be the professional activity which would bring the post-war new Jerusalem of ordered cities and planned environments.

There has been vast amount of literature which has sought to explain, analyse and assess town planning in Britain - planning is arguably the most widely analysed activity of late twentieth century government - and this is particularly true of the last ten years when the traditional values and goals of planning have been brought into question. This literature has focused upon the effects of planning - who gains and who loses; the political economy of planning - in whose interests does planning operate; the organisation of planning; the future of planning, and so on (*e.g.* Kirk, 1980; Ambrose, 1986; Brindley, 1989; Thornley, 1991). In general, these analyses have sought to examine planning, as it were, from the outside - an examination of outcomes, of plans and published documents, of political struggles. In contrast, the planners themselves have hardly been considered at all other than in a rather general and often dismissive way, for example as 'evangelistic bureaucrats' (Davies, 1972). Very little is known about this occupational group in terms of its influence upon the formation and implementation of policies related to the control, management and development of the environment or indeed, in terms of its members' attitudes, values, ethics and perceptions of the role and purpose of the town planning process.

Most writings on these themes originating from within the profession are, perhaps inevitably, un-enlightening, tending to focus, for example, upon the 'technical' constraints on action. In contrast, studies undertaken by social scientists, mostly sociologists, have been uniformly critical of the profession and the way in which it operates. However, most of these studies have tended to concentrate upon either the inadequacies of planning seen as a consequence of the discipline's lack of any kind of coherent theory (Reade, 1987), or to focus upon planning as a function of the state directly serving the needs of capital (Castells, 1977). Little research has been done on the ways in which planners approach their work and the forces which mould their actions in their day to day activities.

This book then, is an attempt to address these issues. It is a study of the profession and activity of town planning in contemporary Britain and as such it is concerned to examine the position of the men and women who earn their living by practising as town planners, in both the public and private sectors, in order to understand how they and their profession can influence decisions about our environment.

But why 'experts' and why 'environmental planning' as the title of this book? Town planners claim to be experts in their field - the business of deciding the 'best' pattern of land use at any particular point in time. This claim is pivotal to an appreciation of the role and function of the town planning profession, and as will become apparent, it is a central argument of this book that an understanding of how knowledge is exploited, codified, created and controlled is a key to an understanding of the public policy process.

'Environmental planning' needs more explanation. That town planning has been is about planning the environment is clear, and it is equally clear that, until about ten years ago, town planners were, unarguably, the 'environmental professionals'. However, during the last decade there has been a major sea-change in both public attitudes towards environmental questions and in public policy responses to the environment. The increasing popularity of the notion of sustainable development following the publication of the Brundtland Report in 1987; the 1992 'Earth Summit' in Rio de Janeiro; the signing of the Maastricht Treaty and the approval of the European Union's Fifth Environmental Action Programme - these and other events have ushered in what has been termed the 'new environmental agenda' of integrated public policy driving towards some conception of sustainability (Agyeman and Evans, 1994).

This new approach to environmental policy making and implementation has been called 'environmental planning' by the Town and Country Planning Association (Blowers, 1993), in order to distinguish it from what might be called traditional or 'classical' town planning. Land use planning is an important and integral part of environmental planning - the integrated and holistic approach to environmental policy making covering a whole range of policy areas such as pollution, water resources, waste management and reclamation and so on - but it is no longer *primus inter pares*, the environmental super-profession directing the activities of the others. In short, the reign of classical town planning, the business of town design, is largely over.

It has been argued elsewhere that this means that a town planning profession is now no longer necessary (if indeed it ever was), and that equally, there is no need for the new professionalisation of 'environmental planning' (Evans, 1993; 1994). The arguments which underpin this position will hopefully become clear as the chapters of this book unfold, since a study of the existing profession charged with land use planning not only helps us understand why and how planners do what they do, but it also provides some indication of what might be required in the future.

However, the study of one occupational group, regardless of how interesting that group may be, is unlikely to reveal information of wider value unless it is located within a broader theoretical framework. This book therefore draws upon a number of theoretical perspectives with two ends in view. Firstly, these perspectives order and inform this investigation of professional planners. They indicate the lines of inquiry to be pursued and the questions to be asked. Secondly, the study of planners is an opportunity to test the validity of some of these propositions with a view to making a contribution towards these theoretical debates.

There are three broad areas of theory which are appropriate here. The first, and perhaps principal area is social class and the substantial body of literature within sociology which is concerned with class analysis. In particular the current debate over the nature of the middle class and the existence of a service class has particular relevance for the study of an occupational group such as planners. As will be seen, there is considerable debate about the composition of the service class, about the extent to which it can be conceived as a cohesive class or not, and how far its members may be viewed as independent of either capital or labour. However, despite this wide-ranging debate, it seems that town planners are a clear example of the kind of occupational group which falls within most conceptions of the service class. In many ways they constitute a classic example - highly credentialised; employed in both the public and private sectors; until very recently in high demand in the employment market; and so on. An examination of this occupational group provides an opportunity to test a number of the key propositions which form part of the service class debate. By the same token, the insights provided by this same debate are invaluable in examining the power and influence of the planners themselves.

The second area of theory is more diffuse and can perhaps best be brought together under the heading of 'public policy theory'. Town planning is primarily a state activity, and the majority of planners are still employed by either central or local government. Consequently, in seeking to explain and assess the role of planners it is useful to draw upon the variety of theoretical perspectives which seek to explain aspects of public policy by examining the attitudes, actions and values of the individual actors in the policy process. Examples of these theoretical perspectives are managerialist theory, corporatist theory and the theoretical perspectives related to bureaucracy and professions. As in the case of the service class, an examination of one particular group may shed light upon the theoretical propositions outlined. This is, of course, an extensive body of literature, and the focus here is not upon all areas of decision making and influence, but primarily on the ways in which 'experts' such as planners can influence and even control policy.

This leads to the third area of theory which is that focused on knowledge and the control and exploitation of expertise. Studies of professionalism and professionalisation can help in an understanding of the ways in which particular occupational groups seek to claim cognitive competency and then exploit control over particular areas of expertise. Moreover, an understanding of the processes whereby knowledge is expropriated and legitimised can be in turn linked to perceptions concerning the ways in which expert labour is controlled or regulated.

Clearly there is a high level of overlap between all these three areas, but this initial definition of starting points makes it easier to specify the theoretical 'tool kit' which will be used to investigate planners, and which in turn will be the subject of some tentative honing as a result. This book will seek to pursue these investigations by firstly considering the issue of class, which is the subject of Chapter 2. Here, the intention is to outline the current debate, focusing on the contributions of Abercrombie, Lash and Urry, Goldthorpe and Wright. Particular attention is given to the 'asset approach' to class analysis and formation developed in the work of Wright and extended by Savage and his colleagues. The purpose of this discussion is to provide a working conceptualisation which will serve to permit an analysis of planners, and to identify propositions which can be assessed in later chapters.

Much of the debate over the service class centres on the notion of credentialisation and the control of expert knowledge. Equally, notions of professionalism involve the allegedly altruistic monopoly of technical knowledge held by certain occupational groups. An appreciation of the ways in which expert labour is used and regulated is fundamental to an understanding of occupational groups such as planners who claim professional status, and to power structures which may arise from the control of such technical knowledge. Chapter 3 therefore considers the nature of expertise in the context of professionalism and professionalisation, bureaucracy and the processes of corporatism.

Chapter 4 utilises the insights of the two previous chapters to examine town planners and the planning system in Britain, focusing particularly on planners as professional experts and members of the middle class. The expert knowledge of planners is examined as is the character of professionalism and the process of professionalisation of planning. This then leads to a consideration of the planners themselves in Chapter 5 by way of an examination of the results of the existing survey material and a report of the findings of a survey of senior Chartered Town Planners carried out mid-1990.

As was mentioned above, although much has been written on the subject of planning generally, very little work has been undertaken examining the planners themselves - for example their values and attitudes, ownership of assets, career patterns, relationship to locality and so on. It was therefore decided to undertake a survey of 500 senior and middle management planners in both the public and private sectors in order to provide an up to date and detailed source of material for the purposes of this study. On the basis of this empirical evidence and the discussions contained in the previous chapters, the final chapter outlines a series of conclusions relating to town planning, professionalism and expert labour, and social class.

2 The debate over the middle class

In the previous chapter it was argued that one crucial area of academic debate which can throw light upon the occupational grouping of town planners is the tradition of class analysis within sociology. The last decade has seen the publication of a substantial number of significant contributions to this debate which have collectively stimulated a lively re-examination by the sociological community of many established views. This chapter seeks to examine that part of this contemporary debate which focuses upon the middle class in general and upon the employed middle class in particular, with a view to establishing theoretical perceptions on these social groupings, and the processes which might form them, as a necessary preliminary to understanding the social and economic positions that town planners and the town planning profession hold.

In many ways, this contemporary 'debate over the middle class' is not difficult to define. Although there have been many studies of social groupings other than the middle class during recent years - those by Crompton and Jones (1984), Scott (1982) and Gorz (1982) for example - a significant number of the books and articles concerned with class and class analysis have chosen to focus upon the middle class (for example Abercrombie and Urry 1983; Carter 1985; Lash and Urry 1988; Scase and Goffee 1982). Moreover, the studies that have sought to present an analysis of the whole class structure have tended to exhibit a focus upon the middle classes or the service class (Goldthorpe 1987; Wright 1985; Marshall, *et al.* 1989).

This concern with what Abercrombie and Urry have described as 'one of the most intractable issues in contemporary sociology' - the position of that class or classes located between capital and labour - can perhaps be seen to be the dominant consideration of sociologists involved in class analysis, whether they adopt a neo-Marxist or a neo-Weberian position, or some approach involving a combination of both of these. Clearly this 'problem of the middle class' derives initially from their intermediate position between the bourgeoisie and the proletariat and from their heterogeneity, which has been compounded by the growing diversity of middle class occupations and by the increase in the number of people within them.

The legacy of Marx and Weber

Before examining the various contemporary perspectives on the middle class, it is necessary to briefly consider the relevance and influence of the Marxist and Weberian traditions. Some writers have argued the antagonistic and mutually exclusive nature of these two traditions. Crompton and Gubbay held that any attempt to synthesise the two concepts of class is 'doomed to failure because of the fundamental differences between the two theorists' (Crompton and Gubbay 1977, p.2). Similarly, Wright emphasised the distinctive character of the two approaches by insisting that; 'At the heart of the distinction between Weberian and Marxist concepts of class, therefore, is the contrast between an essentially culturalist theory of society and history and a materialist theory' (Wright 1985, p.108).

In contrast, other writers have emphasised the need to utilise the insights of both traditions in developing class analysis. Abercrombie and Urry, discussing the middle classes, forcefully argue that 'a separation of Marxist and Weberian theory is not now theoretically profitable and that an adequate theory may well seem eclectic, incorporating and rejecting elements of both approaches' (p.152). Savage, *et al.* argue that this is correct, since both Weberian and Marxist approaches have a common perspective on the middle classes which centres around three elements. Firstly, they both proceed by detecting the dominant structure of contemporary society and then categorise the middle class in terms of the way in which it is functionally tied to serve this dominant feature. Secondly, by knowing the basic and dominant features of society, it is possible to understand the position of the middle classes, and finally, rather than looking at the active formation of middle class groups, the middle class groups are slotted in to class positions created by other agencies, (Savage, *et al.*, 1992).

This mingling of Weberian and Marxist approaches is illustrated further in Marshall, *et al's.* critique of Wright's neo-Marxist analysis of class (Wright 1985; Marshall, *et al.*, 1988). Marshall, *et al.* argue that Wright 'blurs the distinction between Weberian and Marxist accounts of class processes' (although in the same sentence they recognise that this need in no way affect the utility of his substantive analysis, p.48). They base this view on their assessment that Wright 'so emasculates the Marxist theory of history that, taken together with Wright's other concessions to his critics, one is left wondering as to what, precisely, is any longer distinctively Marxist about Wright's account'. A somewhat similar position is taken by Carchedi (1989). Furthermore, Marshall *et al.* accuse Wright of appropriating Weberian perspectives in his use of organisational and skill assets. It is interesting to note, as Savage *et al.* do, that since Marshall and his colleagues are self-declared Weberians, one might therefore expect them to be more sympathetic to Wright's account. However, it is probably more important to recognise the insights to be gained from a less polarised approach to class analysis.

This point is emphasised by the work of writers such as Rattansi (1985) who have argued that the 'classic' Marxist position has in any event been regularly misrepresented, and stereotyped, and that the more sophisticated views of the later Marx legitimated a range of theoretical developments which had been thought to contradict Marx's views as presented in the simple stereotype (see Sarre, 1989 for a discussion). In any event it seems reasonable to suggest that 'Marxist' and 'Weberian' positions are less clearly defined than many might wish. As Marshall *et al.* put it, albeit slightly cynically:

> It is clear, then, that such differences between Marxian and Weberian theory as are conventionally identified - Weber's emphasis on market processes as compared to that placed on the sphere of production by Marx for example - can be magnified or minimised according to which one of the several Marxian and Weberian accounts of class one elects to pursue. At the level of social theory, social classes can be almost all things to all people, most of whom will be able to claim a respectable pedigree for their favoured approach. In practice, therefore, the differences between Marxist and Weberian frameworks are more obvious from the details of research procedure than from the axioms of class theory itself (p.18).

The position on class analysis outlined below (and for that matter the discussions on organisations, bureaucracy, professions and so on developed in subsequent chapters) is based upon the view expressed by Abercrombie and Urry (1983), Sarre (1989), Savage, *et al.* (1992), Burris

(1989) and others that there is no academic profit in seeking to adhere doggedly to one or other of these traditional perspectives. On the contrary, there seems to be much to gain from a thoughtful merging of Marxian and Weberian approaches, particularly through a combination of insights on ownership, authority and market relations.

A reading of Wright's most recent work on class emphasises this when he feels obliged to undertake a spirited defence of Marxism against the 'Weberian Temptation'. However, he concludes that:

> Weberian solutions, therefore, do represent a way of avoiding the conceptual knots generated by trying to conceptualise the middle classes within the Marxist tradition. But these solutions are purchased at the price of lowering the ambitiousness of one's theoretical aspirations and abandoning the attempt at consistency with the conceptual framework - Marxism broadly conceived - that remains the most coherent general approach to radical, emancipatory social theory, (Wright, 1989, p.332).

This is an understandable position given Wright's longstanding commitment to a Marxist analysis of class, although despite this statement, much of his argument in both *Classes* and his later work seems unmistakably Weberian in character, though it is none the worse for that (Wright, 1985, 1989; Marshall *et al.*, 1989). However, from the perspective of this particular study of the profession of planning, Abercrombie and Urry's position is a much more useful starting point:

> In sum it has become increasingly difficult to decide what theory belongs in which camp, and what general rules could establish a privileged discourse. Analysis of the middle class raises this problem particularly acutely. As 'Weberians' have become worried about the Boundary Problem, and 'Marxists' have recognised the importance of the middle classes, the theoretical waters were bound to become muddy. In these circumstances it is more profitable to worry less about the way in which one discourse is privileged over another and more about the manner in which an adequate theory of the middle class can be constructed, (Abercrombie and Urry, 1983, p.91).

Savage, *et al.* (1992) argue that much of this contemporary 'debate' over the middle class from Weberian and Marxist perspectives may be seen as largely redundant if a shift in class analysis from understanding middle class positions to understanding middle class formation is undertaken. They see social classes as social collectivities rooted in particular types of exploitative relationships. Class analysis is therefore concerned to understand the causal properties of different forms of exploitation which may give rise to social collectivities rather than a process which seeks to specify the boundaries of 'actually existing' classes. This leads to their argument that middle class formation is based around three causal entities - the assets of property, bureaucracy and culture

As will be shown below, this 'asset approach' to understanding class formation, and the exploitative relationships involved, is particularly useful for understanding the position of middle class employees, such as town planners. However, before considering this work it is first necessary to review the extensive and influential debate on the service class.

The middle class as a service class?

The concept of the service class derives from the awareness that, in industrial and post-industrial capitalist economies, an occupational category or grouping has emerged located between the traditional proletariat and the bourgeoisie. This class or social category is usually held to contain the expanding occupations of senior professionals, managers and administrators and has been variously conceptualised as the Professional-Managerial Class (Ehrenreichs, 1979), the Salaried Middle Class (Gould, 1981) the New Class (Gouldner, 1979) or more commonly, the Service Class (Abercrombie and Urry, 1983; Lash and Urry, 1989; Goldthorpe, 1982).

All of these writers adopt a position which broadly argues that the classic Marxist conception of a dual model of class conflict is insufficient to account for the emergence of these occupational groups in between capital and labour. They all consider and reject positions which attempt to allocate various fragments of this middle group to either the proletariat or the bourgeoisie, and most argue that this group has some degree of independence from both labour and capital, and also a level of causal power.

The Austro-Marxist Karl Renner is widely credited with the first usage of the notion of a service class (Renner, 1953). He argued that the capitalist is an agent of circulation, and as such makes use of paid assistants who gradually take over his functions.

> These agents are not wage workers; they do not produce, but dispose of the values that have been produced. As long as a capitalist economy exists their services are socially necessary. (Renner, 1953, p.249).

Renner identifies the existence of service class workers in both public and private service and argues that such workers are salaried, not waged and that this reflects the fact that they produce not economic goods, but law and order. A salary establishes a life-style rather than simply providing subsistence, and this life-style improves as the worker ages, terminating in a pension. Moreover, service class relationships with the capitalist depend on trust rather than a labour contract and thus such relationships tend to rest upon a code of service.

According to Renner, until the second world war, the service class was on the borderline between a class and a caste. As a caste this social stratum was recruited from the bourgeois middle class and salaries would be supplemented by income from property. Thus, argues Renner, this caste was both intellectually and materially opposed to the working class. However, as a service class develops in post war Europe, the majority of its members become in practice propertyless and thus 'the service class is closer to the rising working class in its lifestyle, and at its boundaries tends to merge with it', (p.251). Despite this suggestion of the impending proletarianisation of the service class, Renner is offering a clear view of a class, distinct from both capital and labour, which is defined in terms of the services it provides for capital.

The term service class was used by Dahrendorf in the late 1960s, although in a more restricted sense (Dahrendorf, 1969). He argued that the term should be used to describe bureaucrats whose role is to administer and thus act as a link between the rulers and the ruled. In one sense, Dahrendorf agrees with Renner in that both accept the principle of delegation, but Dahrendorf's service class incorporates all workers who are part of a bureaucratic hierarchy, and despite the title, it is therefore not so much a class but more an 'aggregation of ruling groups', (Dahrendorf, 1969). Nevertheless, Dahrendorf's emphasis upon the service class as a bureaucratic class is a perspective which is returned to by later writers.

Goldthorpe and his colleagues have used the category of the service class in the study of social mobility in Britain. Seven social classes were identified, and the first of these containing higher administrative workers and managers, large proprietors and 'free' professionals constitutes a service class (Goldthorpe, 1987). Goldthorpe goes on to argue that the service class is the dominant social grouping of late twentieth century capitalism, that it is increasingly becoming more cohesive and closed off from other social groups, and that it will be more influential in social, economic and political life (Goldthorpe, 1982, 1987). These comments on the service class may be correct, but as Abercrombie and Urry note, Goldthorpe's conception of the service class is principally as a aggregation of occupations, rather than as a class united by the performance of service for capital or a bureaucracy. Also, in contrast to the position of Renner, it is not an intermediate class, but is at the top of a hierarchy (Abercrombie and Urry, p.32).

Goldthorpe's approach is firmly Weberian, and thus there is considerable emphasis upon the processes of class formation in relation to processes of social mobility. This enables Goldthorpe to draw these conclusions on the character of the service class:

> One may say of the service class, as the expanding class of the mid-twentieth century, what Marx said of the industrial proletariat of the mid-nineteenth: that it has been 'recruited from all classes of the population'...... The difference between the two situations is, of course, that while the immobility of the proletariat was the result essentially of constraint - of a lack of opportunity and resources for escape - that of the service class derives rather from the capacity of its members to preserve their position of relative class advantage, (1987, p.333).

This emphasis upon class formation and the capacity of the service class to preserve its privileged position is taken up in the work of Abercrombie and Urry (1983) and Lash and Urry (1987). Goldthorpe's definition of the service class is primarily an occupational one; the categorisation of certain well-paid occupations, based upon work and market situations. He argues that it is increasingly a stabilising, conservative force within modern society, and that the basis of the expanding service class is essentially a bureaucratic one (Goldthorpe, 1987, p.333). In contrast, Urry and his colleagues emphasise the destabilising effect of the service class. Whilst they are concerned with broadly the same occupational categories as Goldthorpe, their approach enables them to perceive the service class not only in terms of its causal powers, but also to understand its historical development in relation to other classes. Thus, for example, for Lash and Urry, the service class in Britain dates from the 1960s, whilst Goldthorpe would presumably see it as existing well before this date. Moreover, whilst Goldthorpe is concerned to develop a class scheme that best 'fits' the reality of social stratification in Britain, Abercrombie and Urry and Lash and Urry are more concerned to understand the emergence of the service class in an historical context (the process of class formation) and to specify the role and function of the service class within capitalism, and thus they more directly follow Renner's original conception of the service class.

Abercrombie and Urry draw upon both the Marxist and Weberian traditions to draw four major conclusions about the 'middle class' and the service class in modern capitalist societies. Firstly they argue that a separation of Marxist and Weberian theory is not now theoretically profitable, and that even though there are difficulties in adequately separating the two positions, an eclectic position is tenable. This leads them to argue that social classes should be:

a seen as sets of social relationships connecting together places within the social division of labour,

b conceptualised in terms of market and work situations, and,

c seen as involving important processes of recruitment which in part affect the structuring of such places.

Secondly, this leads them to conclude that the 'middle class' in Britain must be seen as two classes, the service class and deskilled routine white collar workers, defined by their different market and work situations and their different functions. The service class has taken on and concentrated within itself the functions of capital, namely conceptualisation, control and reproduction. In contrast, the deskilled white collar workers are being proletarianised and therefore cannot be properly seen as 'middle class'. However, they also point out that it may be equally inaccurate to perceive the service class as 'middle class' in that its functions are delegated from capital and thus, historically speaking, from the capitalist class.

Thirdly, Abercrombie and Urry argue that a new and relatively unrecognised process within the development of capitalism is the socialisation of unproductive labour:

> Because of the transformed relationship of labour and knowledge in contemporary capitalism, places within the social division of labour are crucially structured by different educational requirements: in particular, white-collar places are distinguished from the service class in terms of the different credentials demanded. And, at the same time, the process of class formation, of the recruitment of persons to places, is increasingly the outcome

> of the distribution of hierarchically ordered educational credentials to such persons, (p.153).

Finally, classes must be seen as possessing powers to produce empirical outcomes, and in the case of the service class in modern capitalist societies, these powers have become considerably enhanced:

> ... powers reflected in various kinds of economic, political and social struggles which have increased the development of the socialisation of unproductive labour, forced mental and manual labour further apart, increased the credentialisation of both places and persons, concentrated capital functions within the service class, deskilled the white collar labour process, separated the service class from deskilled white collar workers in respect of their market and work situations, and transformed the political position of labour. They have, in other words, transformed the very structure within which the service class is to be seen as a 'class-in-struggle', (p.153).

These conclusions represent a considerable reappraisal of the notion of the service class, giving major significance to the class in developed capitalist economies, and providing a theoretical structure within which this class can be assessed. In the final paragraph of Abercrombie and Urry's book is a recognition that the position and power of the service class will vary between capitalist societies, and this theme is taken up in Lash and Urry's work along with an examination of the development of the service class in Britain (Lash and Urry, 1987).

Lash and Urry argue that the emergence of the service class must be understood in the context of 'organised capitalism', where it was generated and developed out of the relationship between labour and capital. However, once it attains a certain threshold of development and mobilisation, this new class itself begins to have a dislocating effect on the relationship between capital and labour and an 'irredeemably disorganising effect on capitalist society in general'.

Lash and Urry go on to specify a number of central points about the service class. They argue that it consists of those dominant positions or places within the social division of labour which do not principally involve the ownership of capital, land or buildings. These places are located within a set of interlocking social institutions that 'service' capital through meeting three functions which are to conceptualise the labour process; to control the entry and exercise of labour power within the workplace; and to orchestrate the non-household forms under which labour power is produced and regulated.

The service class consists of those places which enjoy superior work and market situations. Incumbents thus exercise authority within each institution, typically enjoying well-defined 'careers' in which work and market situations improve side by side. They also enjoy medium to high levels of trust and discretion often stemming from forms of professional control and closure. Entry into such places is generally regulated by the differential possession of credentials, which are either organisation-specific or are general, and these credentials serve as the main demarcation between the service class and deskilled white collar workers. Finally, the relative size, the power, and the composition (male/female, public/private) of the service class will vary substantially, depending upon class conflicts between capital and labour; gender conflicts, (particularly over attempts to professionalise/masculinise occupations); struggles to extend educational credentialism; attempts to 'professionalise' particular sets of work tasks; conflicts over the size, functions and organisation of the state; sectoral changes in the national economy, and so on. (p.162).

For Lash and Urry, the service class must be understood as a class which developed in conjunction with the emergence of 'knowledge, education and science'. This leads them to argue the centrality of the development of modern scientific rational management to twentieth century capitalism. This development was not inevitable, but was closely bound up with the social relations between capital and labour in particular societies. In America, for example, they argue that there was something of a class struggle at the beginning of the twentieth century between existing capital and 'modern management'.

Lash and Urry demonstrate how scientific management became established in the United States in the early part of this century. In Britain, however, a different pattern emerged. The 'progressivism' that existed in the United States in this period was absent in Britain, and the introduction of scientific management was resisted. This resistance was related to the development of two 'preferred agents' of management within British industry - the 'educated amateur' or the 'gentleman' and the 'practical man'. As a consequence of this resistance, scientific management did not develop in Britain at the same time as in the United States, and thus no service class developed until the 1960's. When it did develop, the British service class was very much dominated by the development of the 'welfare state' and the associated expansion of professional and managerial occupations within the state.

They emphasise that 'knowledge' has been significantly appropriated away from the working class and embodied within the institutions of science, the professions and education, the directors of which constitute a class which serves capital but increasingly does so on its own terms. As a consequence, the causal powers of the working class have been progressively weakened as that class is subject to control and reproduction by the service class. Moreover, this control of knowledge means that the power of the service class appears to be legitimate since their work is premised upon 'technical rationality'.

Lash and Urry argue that the service class does not necessarily have interests coincidental with those of 'capital', and that much contemporary politics is organised around divisions **within** the service class, or conflicts between sections of that class and capital. In particular, they see a major division between the public and private wings of the service class, the relative power of the former having a major effect on the character and strength of socialist and social democratic politics in each society. Much labourist or social democratic struggle, whether of manual workers or deskilled white collar workers, is directed against the 'service class' rather than against the capitalist class itself: the latter is anyway becoming 'depersonalised' and less obviously a target for political contestation.

They conclude that the potential oppositional groupings to 'capital' are 'nevertheless exceedingly large'. Many sectors of the service class organise to protect their interests and they will struggle very hard to preserve gains made or to extend those gains. Such groupings will use a variety of organisational means - profession, trade union or voluntary association - and their struggles often involve opposition to capital and/or the state. Finally, they argue that the service class has been partly responsible for generating new 'social movements', not directly structured by the relations of production, and these have led to the redrawing of boundaries of social division, political conflict, and cultural experience.

This conceptualisation of the service class offers a range of insights and propositions which have a direct bearing upon the circumstances of a credentialised, public sector occupational group such as town planners. Subsequent chapters will discuss these ideas further, but is it first necessary to examine the work of Wright, and the development of the 'asset approach' to class analysis.

The class theories of E.O. Wright

The opening paragraphs of this chapter noted that the last decade has witnessed a spirited debate within sociology over the nature of class and class formation, and in major part this has been dominated by the neo-Weberian analysis of Goldthorpe and the neo-Marxist approach of Wright (Goldthorpe, 1982, 1987; Wright, 1979, 1985 and 1989). In his book *Classes* (1985), Wright argues that classes in capitalist society should be seen as rooted in the complex intersection of three forms of exploitation; exploitation based on the ownership of capital assets, the control of organisation assets and the possession of skill or credential assets. This formulation permits him to address the 'embarrassment of the middle classes' in that he perceives them as being in contradictory class locations within 'actually existing capitalism'. That is to say, they may occupy contradictory locations in exploitation relations in that they are simultaneously exploiters and exploited. As Wright points out, this situation applies to a substantial proportion of the population in the advanced capitalist countries who are in neither of the categories of proletariat or bourgeoisie. Thus, he argues;

> ... instead of regarding all positions as located uniquely within particular classes and thus having a coherent class character in their own right, we should see some positions as possibly having a multiple class character; they may be in more than one class simultaneously, (1989, p.43).

In emphasising the exploitation centred concept of class, Wright is utilising the work of Roemer (1982) who challenges the traditional Marxist definition of class relations primarily in terms of domination within the sphere of production. He argues that the notion of exploitation is a more revealing way of understanding inequalities in capitalist societies in that the concept of exploitation reflects the existence of a particular kind of causal relationship between groups and actors in society. Thus, in Roemer's analysis, as in the traditional Marxist concept of exploitation through the expropriation of surplus value, exploitation occurs when the welfare of one group depends upon the deprivations of another. Roemer elaborates this view by utilising the concept of 'assets' - physical assets (alienable assets) and skill assets (inalienable assets) - which have exploitation-generating qualities and which form the basis of exploitative class relationships.

Wright develops Roemer's position into a general theory of class which is centred on the exploitation of the three assets mentioned above

- capital assets, organisation assets and skill assets. Wright suggests that each of these assets may be seen as having particular prominence in different 'class structures' or modes of production. Thus the principal assets that are unequally distributed in capitalism are capital assets; in 'statism' (referring to state socialist societies) it is organisational assets; while in socialism it is skill assets (Wright, 1985, p.83).

Wright's approach has been subject to wide criticism, most notably in Britain by Marshall, *et al.* (1988) who, after an exhaustive empirical study conclude that Wright's formulation and class categories do not fit the reality revealed by empirical research in Britain. However, as Savage, *et al.* point out, (1992) to judge class theories principally by statistical criteria - which has the best statistical measure of association, and by implication fewer 'boundary problems' - is to adhere to a view of class that is terminally limiting. Other writers have criticised his economic determinism and his effective rejection of many fundamental principles of Marxism (see Wright, 1989, for a review of these criticisms and Wright's response).

Nevertheless, despite the wide reservations that have been expressed, his conception of exploitation based upon the ownership or control of assets appears a useful starting point for the examination of the middle classes. Savage, *et al.* (1992) take this view and combine these perspectives with insights drawn from the writings of Bourdieu whose work is briefly considered next.

Bourdieu and cultural capital

Bourdieu's book *Distinction: a Social Critique on the Judgement of Taste,* (1984) was introduced into the debate on class analysis in Britain by Lash and Urry (1987). The book is an analysis of class, taste and lifestyle in France, and as such there must be reservations over the applicability of all of his conclusions to the somewhat different culture of Britain. Nevertheless, his observations on the middle class (or 'dominant class') are useful. He argues that a distinction may be drawn within the dominant class between 'intellectuals' (artists and higher education teachers) and the 'bourgeoisie', and that this distinction is based upon control and ownership of two distinct kinds of capital, economic capital and cultural capital. Intellectuals are high on cultural capital, but possess little economic capital, while the bourgeoisie are high on economic capital but weak on cultural capital. Bourdieu defines other, subsidiary classes, but what is distinctive about Bourdieu's work is not his classification of class structure, but his contribution to the debate on class formation, in that he sees economic and cultural capital as resources which people use to reproduce themselves in certain social positions. It is a way of thinking about the reproduction of social inequality which does not link it to the structure of employment.

Of course, the concept of cultural capital has been used by other writers in the debate on class analysis. For example both Gouldner (1979) and Gould (1981) specifically refer to the concept and point to its significance in both class formation and processes of social closure, and in many ways their use of the concept appears to be very similar to that of Bourdieu. The main difference seems to be Bourdieu's insistence on the processes of legitimation, whereby cultural capital is made legitimate as a result of struggles between different classes. However, this process of struggle and legitimation is not really explained by Bourdieu and it is unclear how the process actually unfolds.

Nevertheless, Bourdieu does offer several useful insights which are pertinent to this study of planners. In particular, his notion of "habitus" is a useful device for representing the community of interest and experiences shared by particular groups. In the case of the middle class this is exemplified in the work of Dearlove (1973) who showed that middle class residents' groups were more successful in achieving their aims than working class groups because the former were able to establish a "reasonable and rational" dialogue with council officers and elected members. This was based upon a shared understanding and acceptance of certain values and principles - in Bourdieu's terms, a common habitus.

Bourdieu's utilization of the concepts of cultural capital and economic capital to an extent reflect the 'asset approach' of Wright. However Bourdieu emphasises the way in which these assets may be interchanged - economic capital may be used to secure cultural capital and vice versa. Although Wright recognises that this may occur, Bourdieu sees this interchangeability of assets as central. This will be returned to later in the context of judging the assets that town planners may exploit.

Assets and class formation

The work of Savage and his colleagues (1988; 1992) draws firstly upon that of Wright and then Bourdieu to construct an original perspective on the middle class and its formation and for reasons that will become apparent, this is best described as the 'asset approach' to class analysis.

Savage, Dickens and Fielding (1988) argue that the concept of the service class is far too inclusive:

> ... since it conflates different types of top level workers who have very different relationships with other social groups. Far from there being an increasingly cohesive service class, we believe that there is growing fragmentation at the top of the social hierarchy which is only clouded by continued reference to a service class, (Savage, *et al.*, p.457).

They go on to argue that one growing division is the development of the 'new' service class working in small firms or self employed, which has emerged particularly during the last decade, and which now must be seen as standing alongside the 'traditional' service class based in the public sector or in large companies.

Savage, *et al.* draw upon Wright's formulation of class to further develop this position. Wright argues that class relations are based upon the possession of particular kinds of assets. These may be capital assets (for investment), organisation assets (resulting from a position in an organisation) and skill assets (possession of a scarce skill). Savage, *et al.* argue that a distinction may be made between the traditional service class and the new service class which is a distinction between groups possessing organisation assets (the traditional service class concentrated in large organisations in both the public and private sectors) and skill assets (the new service class self employed or in small firms). They conclude that these two sectors of the service class are likely to have different geographical patterns of distribution in Britain, and are likely to have different political perspectives, particularly with respect to locality politics and matters of conservation.

This position is further developed in more recent work by Savage and his colleagues (Savage, *et al.*, 1992). In this book they develop the approach outlined in the earlier article by firstly insisting on the significance of class formation as opposed to class structure; secondly by emphasising the historical character of class, and thirdly by arguing the centrality of the three assets of property (economic), bureaucracy (organisation) and culture (skill assets/cultural capital) as the causal entities of middle class formation.

They argue that the purpose of class analysis is not to register strong measures of statistical association between social classes and other social practices: rather it is to throw light on the dynamics of social change, through analyses of social division and cleavage. Thus, they argue that much of the 'debate' on the middle class is unhelpful because it has tended to focus upon the structure of middle class positions rather than emphasising the processes of middle class formation. This distinction follows the separation of 'places' from 'persons' (Poulantzas, 1978) and reflects the contention that while class structure refers to the system of positions in the division of labour, class formation refers to the way in which these groups of people who occupy a common place in the social division of labour may form as a social collectivity on the basis of these positions.

This distinction reflects the Weberian position that class action is not inevitable (as Marxists might claim), and that classes 'are not communities, they merely reflect possible and frequent bases for communal action', (Gerth and Mills, 1948, p.181). The notion of class formation is also central to Goldthorpe's (neo-Weberian) analysis in that he sees it as inextricably linked to patterns of social mobility - the longer individuals remain in one social class, the more likely they will be to develop some sense of class allegiance.

In emphasising the importance of examining the processes of class formation at the expense of class structure, Savage, *et al.* recognise the critique of this class structure/class formation divide which holds that class places cannot be specified independently of the people who fill those places. Some positions are defined by the gender of the people doing the job (Crompton and Sanderson, 1990) while as Anthias shows, the nature of a class position tends to change as a racial minority group moves into it (Anthias, 1990). Savage, *et al.* thus propose that class formation must be understood in its historical context, since it may be argued that it is only in certain historical events, or in certain social circumstances that class division become important, and that in many everyday practices social class may not be all that salient. They argue that, following Przeworski (1977), class formation must be seen as the process of organisation, disorganisation and re-organisation of class positions. The process is theoretically prior to, and determinant of, the structure of class positions.

Drawing specifically upon the work of Wright and Bourdieu, Savage, *et al.* link their emphasis upon class formation with three assets or axes of exploitation around which, they argue, middle class formation occurs. The first axis is that of property, which is the least problematic asset in that most writers agree that it exists. The asset of capital is a non-disputed category in that ownership of capital may be clearly identified as conferring advantages and as forming the basis for exploitative social relationships.

The second axis is formed around organisation assets, although this is a more problematic and contested conception. Wright argued that organisation assets;

> ... consist in the effective control over the co-ordination and integration of the division of labour. Typically, such assets are particularly salient in defining the exploitation relations of management, although not all jobs which are formally labelled 'manager' involve control over organisational assets, (Wright, 1985, p.151).

In capitalist societies, Wright argues, organisation assets are generally controlled by managers and capitalists, whereas in statist (or state socialist) societies organisation assets assume a much greater importance because the whole technical division of labour becomes a societal task organised at the centre. Bureaucratic power therefore is control over (but not ownership of) organisation assets, and for Wright this is principally found in the public rather than the private sector. Savage, *et al.*, have, quite correctly, expressed reservations over Wright's usage of organisation assets, principally that he does not adequately differentiate them from his third category of skill assets, and that he ties organisation assets to the public sector when they may be more significant in the private sector.

Wright's third category of asset is based upon skills. Like his category of organisational assets, this has been widely criticised, and Wright himself has recognised the problems inherent in his formulation. In particular, Wright has been at pains to emphasise that although;

> ... the ownership of skill assets, particularly when institutionalised in the form of credentials, may constitute a basis for exploitation. It is much less clear that it should be treated as the basis of a class relation except insofar as skills or credentials might enable one to gain access to other kinds of assets. (Wright, 1989, p.22).

This is because the idea of skill-based classes is less relational than the idea of capital-based classes - there is no inherent social relation which binds skill-owners to the unskilled.

Nevertheless, Wright is clear that both skill assets and organisation assets are what he terms 'secondary exploitations' and are best viewed as the basis for strata (or fractions) within classes rather than for class divisions as such. Such strata, however, can constitute the material basis for the emergence of distinct class trajectories as individuals turn the surplus appropriated through 'credential rents' into capital investment (Wright, 1989, p.347). Thus, for Wright, skill or credential assets are a way of understanding the position of experts within the middle class, although he notes it is this group which has caused him (and other Marxists) 'persistent difficulty' (Wright, 1989, p.331). As Savage, *et al.* point out, Marxism in general has less difficulty in theorising the class position of supervisors and managers than 'experts' and 'professionals' (Savage, *et al.*, 1992).

In general, Savage, *et al.* are unhappy with Wright's use of skill assets as a third axis for class formation. They point out that it is knowledge and specifically, legitimate knowledge, which is the 'asset' here rather than the more general conception of skills. Thus, using Bourdieu, they argue that the third axis of class formation should be more properly identified as state legitimated cultural capital. The social production of legitimate knowledge by organisations - notably the state - produces a corpus of knowledge which can be used to sustain advantaged class positions. The cost is to tie this class to the structures of the state and the power relations implicit within it.

Savage, *et al.* do not claim that it is possible to 'read off' three distinct middle classes, each relying principally on one of these three assets. However, they do argue for the 'historic centrality' of the division between a professional and managerial middle class in Britain (each exploiting these assets differentially) and furthermore, they suggest that current trends may now be undermining this division, replacing it with a broad split between a professional and a propertied middle class.

Before moving to an assessment of this discussion of class analysis in the context of the profession of town planning, it is necessary to briefly consider the relationship which exists between class and locality. The last decade has seen a resurgence of interest in locality issues in social science generally, and there is now an extensive body of literature which seeks to examine the spatial dimensions of class (*e.g.* Dickens, 1988; Cooke, 1989; Bagguley, *et al.*, 1990). It is not necessary to review this literature here, but there are several issues which have emerged as part of the service class debate which justify examination.

Savage, *et al.*, (1988) have argued that different sections of the service class may have different levels of attachment to locality in that, they argue, the new skill-based service class is less likely to be geographically mobile, and thus more likely to be committed to the areas where they live. In contrast, the traditional service class, relying principally upon organisation assets, need to be geographically mobile in order to secure career advancement, and are thus less likely to be committed to their locality. This is an interesting proposition in that it postulates that the reliance upon one or other asset may condition an individual's or a group's attitude to locality, in terms of preparedness to participate in voluntary organisations for example. Although most of the recent literature on 'community' and locality-based social relationships recognises the likelihood of middle-class individuals creating and establishing their own local social worlds at the expense of working-class residents, the suggestion that this should be done principally by certain types of middle-class people is new (Willmott, 1986). Given the importance of careers to the definition of service class occupations, the links between career movements, residential mobility and attachment to locality are worthy of study, and thus these issues will be examined further in Chapter 5.

Class analysis and the profession of town planning

Given the foregoing review of the recent debates on class analysis, what conceptualisations and theoretical positions can be employed to inform this study of one occupational group? For the purposes of this study, Lash and Urry's conception of the service class offers considerable insights. The emphasis upon the use of the concept of the service class to analyse processes of historical change, the perception of the service class as an active political force with a capacity to effect social and economic change, and the awareness of substantial differing sectoral interests within the class all combine to make their conception of this class more useful than Goldthorpe's. However, their approach does have some shortcomings.

An immediate problem stems from their definition of the service class as occupying those places;

> ... located within a set of interlocking social institutions that 'service' capital through meeting three functions: to conceptualise the labour process; to control the entry and exercise of labour power within the workplace; and to orchestrate the non-household forms under which labour power is produced and regulated, (Lash and Urry, p.162).

On this basis many occupations which would be included in Renner's, Dahrendorf's and Goldthorpe's service classes would be excluded, not least the profession of town planning. It would not be difficult to argue that the profession and activity of planning has the function of servicing capital, and it is unclear why the definition is so restrictive.

Crompton takes this point further. In making the point that their definition of the service class hardly describes the full range of service class activities ('what about cultural production, the processes of government and decision-making, sports and entertainment?'), she argues that their account of this class is too narrowly focused in respect of both its emergence and its causal power.

> There is a constant tendency in their account to discuss industrial management as a proxy for the 'service class' as a whole, (Crompton, 1990a, p.7).

Savage, *et al.* emphasise the importance of the process of service class formation in Lash and Urry's work. However, they argue that since they do not specify the economic axes around which the service class secures its own advantage at the expense of other classes, they fail to consolidate their important insights (Savage, *et al.*, 1991). Nevertheless, despite these significant criticisms, this approach has insights which will be returned to in later chapters.

In general though, the conception of the service class must be viewed as having limitations, and these are highlighted by the way in which the concept can be uncritically used to describe all middle class positions with an assumption that there is high degree of cultural and political homogeneity (for example Cloke and Thrift, 1990). It is clear that there is a high degree of diversity within this putative class and it may well be that both 'organising' and 'disorganising' tendencies may be present. Moreover, the emphasis upon expert knowledge and organisations in definition of the class raises further questions over the exact nature of divisions within the service class (Crompton, 1990a, 1990b). Thus, the position that will be taken here is that the concept of the service class as utilised by Lash and Urry will form the basis for an investigation of the occupational grouping of town planners, although this will be substantially conditioned by the 'asset approach' and the literature on professions, organisations, occupations and corporatism, which will be considered in subsequent chapters. This conditional usage of a contested concept is appropriate in the sense that in deciding to reject completely the concept of the service class, for the reasons indicated above, there is a real danger of throwing the theoretical baby out with the bath water. To retain the concept of the service class, albeit conditionally, is to retain a useful heuristic tool.

However, it is clear that the diversity within the service class requires explanation and analysis, and the 'asset approach' of Wright and Savage and his colleagues may provide a framework for this. The use of organisation assets and cultural capital (including skills and credentials) as axes for class formation permits a focus upon how particular sets of middle class groupings or occupations manage to achieve and maintain privileged positions without obviously possessing significant amounts of capital (or economic assets). Linked to an understanding that class, or at least the existence of a 'class for itself', may only occur at particular points in time, in response to particular historical conditions, this perspective allows an examination of middle class formation through a consideration of the particular circumstances pertaining in the case of one particular group.

Yet, there are difficulties with this, not least in the definition and conceptualisation of the assets or axes. Organisation assets pose particular difficulties. In part they may be seen as a focus for the exploitative relationship between super-ordinate and subordinate employees within an organisation, and in this sense the control of organisation assets is largely indistinguishable from the exercise of hierarchical authority (Burris, 1989). It is therefore difficult to see how the super-ordinate employee is able to translate this exploitation into some kind of tangible value transferred out of the work organisation.

In contrast, it is much easier to comprehend how controllers of organisation assets might manipulate the decision making process to pursue their own specific interests or the interests of their particular social grouping, although this perception does tend to move the analysis of organisation assets towards some kind of 'urban managerialist' approach (Pahl, 1975). Similarly, it might be possible to understand organisation assets in terms of Gould's view of the salaried middle class who are able to manipulate state action and expenditure to benefit their own interests (Gould, 1981).

Both of these positions emphasise how middle class public sector workers can utilise their bureaucratic position (or organisation assets) to further their own class interests. Savage, *et al.* disagree, arguing that it is in the private sector rather than the public sector that these assets have paramount importance, although this is tending to decline. In contrast, they argue, public sector workers are much more dependent upon state legitimated cultural capital - knowledge which is produced and legitimised by the state and which can be used as a resource to sustain an advantaged class position.

This position, drawing upon Bourdieu, is using the notion of cultural capital in a very specific sense by relating it specifically to legitimate knowledge, and by association, to the concepts of credentialisation, professionalism, expert labour and corporatism. It seems clear that an examination of all these, and the linkages between them, can throw light upon the profession of town planning. Moreover, by examining this occupational group in detail it may be possible to identify more precisely what cultural capital actually consists of, how it is formed and how it might be transferred into other assets, principally economic assets. In addition, since town planners work in both the public and private sectors, it should be possible to see how far cultural capital has significance for those in private sector organisations.

However, it may be that Savage and his colleagues are incorrect in de-emphasising the significance of organisation assets for public sector workers. Certainly, the experience of the decade 1980-90 might provide evidence to support their contention, but different economic and political conditions could conceivably create circumstances where the balance between organisation assets and cultural capital shifts, and public sector organisation assets become more important as, for example, public expenditure increases. Thus, assessing the relative importance of these two assets for the public and private sectors will be one of the goals of subsequent chapters, as will an attempt to define more precisely the character, form and significance of both organisation assets and cultural capital.

The next chapter begins this process by examining the relationship between expert labour and power, with a view to establishing how the ownership and control of expert knowledge can be understood and how it can contribute to the achievement of privileged positions in society. This discussion will therefore consider how organisation assets and cultural capital can be conceptualised in the context of expert labour, and will form the starting point for a consideration of the planning profession in Chapter Four.

3 Expert labour and power

In the previous chapter it was argued that the 'asset approach' to class contained in the work of Wright and Savage and his colleagues offers a useful perspective for analysing the contemporary British middle class, and particularly the credentialised, 'professional' occupational groups such as town planners. An assessment of the way in which particular occupational groups might exploit economic, organisation and skill assets or cultural capital may permit a clearer perception of the processes of middle (or service) class formation. However, the precise nature of these assets or axes has not been fully specified. Although there is no real conceptual problem in the case of economic assets, since these refer, in Wright's terms to 'assets in means of production', the exact composition of organisation assets and skill assets is less clear, and the notion of 'cultural capital' is murkier still.

This chapter seeks to examine the character of these assets by looking at the way in which various occupational groups have managed to secure favourable positions in society either by claiming exclusive control over a certain body of technical or theoretical knowledge, or by utilising organisational or bureaucratic structures to pursue their interests. It is, therefore, a discussion of the way in which expert labour (conceived of in the most general sense, and not just as 'professional') secures and maintains power, and as such it reflects the argument made by Bell and other 'post-industrial' writers that power follows knowledge, and that the political importance of knowledge is growing (Lane, 1966; Bell, 1974).

This discussion is particularly salient for an understanding of a 'welfare' or 'organisational' profession such as town planning (Larson, 1977; Wilding, 1982). As will be seen in the next Chapter, the activity and profession of town planning is overwhelmingly state sponsored and the majority of planners (approximately 80%) work for central and local government bodies. Planners claim to be 'experts' (though the focus of this expertise is open to debate) and 'professionals', and by virtue of their circumstances of employment, most of them are 'bureaucrats'.

Within sociology there is, of course, a well-established body of literature and debate which can inform this discussion - the work on professions, bureaucracy and organisations come immediately to mind. However, it is equally important to place these insights into the context of the debates on political power and policy formulation. In what ways can experts influence or even determine state policy and action? Academic studies of policy and the literature on corporatism can provide some insights here. The remainder of this chapter will therefore seek to examine the nature of expert labour and its relationship to power as a preliminary to considering town planning in the following chapter.

The nature of expert labour

As Abercrombie and Urry point out, where analysis is undertaken of the connections between class and knowledge, attention is directed to the way in which different social classes generate different knowledge-contents. However, they argue, this is too simple in that 'knowledges' provide the very conditions under which classes may exist or develop - for example the service class. This leads them to argue that:

> Hence, classes based on 'educated labour' do not merely generate particular contents of such knowledge. Rather the development of such classes transforms existing class relations because their very formation depends upon the possession of particular kinds of knowledge. And this means that the knowledge has been appropriated away from the direct producers. This appropriation, moreover, means that various knowledges are systematised in the form of different sciences and promulgated through education, and it is these processes which enable labour to be more effectively exploited as a routine, regular and systematic feature of capitalist relations. (Abercrombie and Urry, 1983, p.92).

Knowledge is therefore seen as an axis of class formation. However, the assumption that knowledge has been appropriated away from the direct producers is more problematic. In the case of the development of

Taylorian scientific management, the argument seems plausible in that a central proposition of Taylorism was the removal of 'brain work' from the shop floor to a 'planning room' where managers would perform tasks previously undertaken by manual operatives. However, it is less easy to see how this appropriation might take place in the case of knowledge related to areas of scientific enquiry, such as physics, or professional areas such as psychiatry or traffic engineering. Nevertheless, it is clear that knowledge generally, and 'legitimate' knowledge in particular has become the preserve of particular classes or occupations, and that in general, to control knowledge is to control a resource or asset which can be exploited. It may well be argued that this need not always be the case, and Sohn-Rethel's work is directed towards constructing a theory of knowledge in Marxism, since this is an essential precondition for recombining mental and manual labour in a classless society (Sohn-Rethel, 1978).

Expertise is usually understood as a conferred quality donated by other groups for their own purposes (Gerver and Bensman, 1953). Normally this means that experts have expertise in an area of 'legitimate knowledge', that is, an area of knowledge which is sanctioned, approved or sponsored by the state. As Wilding points out:

> On its own, expertise does not bring power - it has to be useful expertise which is valued by government, and it has to provide guarantees that it will be used only for achieving acceptable purposes in acceptable ways. (Wilding, 1982 p.75).

This, of course, is the basis of professionalisation, which will be discussed in more detail below. Nevertheless, it is also important to recognise the significance of what Parsons called 'the primacy of cognitive rationality', referring to societal faith in the value and importance of expertise and those who possess it, whether they seek professional status or not. In short, there is a faith in knowledge, which in turn underpins the power of those who lay claim to it (Parsons, 1949). Knowledge and expertise is usually legitimated through qualifications or credentials, and as Parkin and others have pointed out, credentialism may be viewed as an exclusionary process of social closure (Abercrombie and Urry 1983; Parkin, 1979). Parkin argues that:

> ... it is necessary to regard credentialism as a form of exclusionary social closure comparable in its importance for class formation to the institution of property. Both entail the use of exclusionary rules that confer benefits and privileges on the few through denying

access to the many, rules that are enshrined in law and upheld by the coercive authority of the modern state. (Parkin, 1979, p.58).

In contrast, Savage argues that it is more accurate to see credentialism as an employer strategy designed to open up 'service class' jobs to workers without long term experience, thus resolving shortages of managerial labour (Savage, 1989).

It is also important to recognise the existence of what Bourdieu refers to as 'epistemic communities', that is collectivities of individuals who share a common knowledge (Bourdieu, 1988). Such communities are likely to be characterised by agreement on what constitutes relevant and accepted knowledge and will make judgments about the relevance and epistemological acceptability of new knowledge. Although Bourdieu is concerned principally with the academic world, the conception has obvious utility in a wider context, particularly in the study of professions, where 'practice' and 'academic' functions both exist.

Professionalism and professionalisation

Profession, as Larson points out:

> ... appears to be one of the many 'natural concepts' fraught with ideology, that social science abstracts from everyday life, (Larson, 1977).

It is not surprising therefore, to find that many of the early sociological writings on the professions tended to reflect and implicitly support the ideology of professionalism and that these 'trait' approaches to the study of the professions have been subsequently widely criticised (Johnson, 1972; Larson, 1977; Wilding, 1982).

Broadly, the trait approach refers to those writings which have sought to identify the characteristics which discriminate between professions and non-professions, the best-known examples being the work of Millerson (1964) and Greenwood (1965). According to this analysis, professions are occupations with a series of particular distinguishing characteristics which in turn determine the superior position and status that professionals generally hold in society. As Larson points out:

> The list of specific attributes which compose the ideal-type of profession may vary, but there is substantial agreement about its

general dimensions. The Cognitive dimension is centred on the body of knowledge and techniques which the professionals apply in their work, and on the training necessary to master such knowledge and skills; the normative dimension covers the service orientation of professionals, and their distinctive ethics, which justify the privilege of self-regulation granted them by society; the evaluative dimension implicitly compares professions to other occupations, underscoring the professions' singular characteristics of autonomy and prestige. The distinctiveness of the professions appears to be founded on the combination of these general dimensions. (Larson, 1977 p.x).

Johnson argues that this approach is fundamentally flawed in that it is both a theoretical and a historical. Within trait theory there is no prior and explicit theoretical framework to determine which characteristics might be important and why, and thus, argues Johnson, trait theory too easily falls into the error of accepting the professionals' own definitions of themselves (Johnson, 1972). Moreover, trait theory is a historical because it assumes the universality of professionalism, whereas it is clear that professionalism is characteristic of Anglo-American culture at a particular point in time (Rueschmeyer, 1983). This is an important point in that trait theory does not consider the general social and economic conditions under which professionalisation occurs. Instead the defining characteristics are taken to be both the cause and the effect of professionalism - the claims for professional status made by the professions themselves are assumed to be the major conditions for professionalism.

Most recent writers on professionalism and professionalisation such as Johnson (1972), Larson (1977), and Friedson (1983), reject trait theory and functionalist perspectives on professionalism, preferring instead to direct their focus towards the processes through which various occupational groups achieve professional status - the process of professionalisation. As Laffin rightly points out:

> the interesting questions about professionalism are those relating to the process of professionalisation. (Laffin, 1986, p.21).

The definition of occupational characteristics is secondary to the question of how particular occupational groups relate to social and political power centres at particular points in time, and how, through these relationships they are able to secure privileged, autonomous conditions of work.

Professionalism on the other hand has been increasingly viewed as a form of occupational control - in Johnson's famous phrase, a 'profession is not, then, an occupation, but a means of controlling an occupation' (Johnson, 1972, p.45). Moreover, it is but one form or order of control which has arisen at a particular historical juncture in particular societies. Other examples would include oligarchic and corporate patronage or state mediation (Johnson, 1972, p.46). The point is that particular forms of expert labour which perform essential services for society or for influential sections of society, need to be controlled or regulated in some way or another, since by definition, clients are likely to be vulnerable in their relationships with professionals.

Crompton (1990a) argues that one possible way to achieve consumer or client protection is to 'demystify' or 'deskill' expert labour by breaking skills down or by subjecting them to some kind of monitoring, routinisation or direct regulation. For example, it might be argued that the introduction of computer technology to construction processes in the building industry will have the effect of deskilling or reducing the professional role of experts such as Quantity Surveyors - the need to manually 'take-off' the quantities of building materials from architects' drawings to price contracts is removed as more and more architects turn to computer-aided design which can provide this service as part of the package. In reality, of course, as Crompton points out 'the destruction of old skills, often involves the creation of new ones, and a stable situation is unlikely to be permanently achieved. The client (purchaser) therefore, will always be at risk of some vulnerability in relation to the expert'.

This leads Crompton to conclude that two major patterns of moral regulation of the circumstances within which expert labour may be exchanged can be identified, and that these patterns stem both from purchasers and from the experts themselves. The first pattern is 'professionalism' which is articulated largely at the level of the occupation, while the second is organisational corporatism or the 'clan form' which is articulated largely at the level of the organisation.

Professionalism is equated with Merton's institutionalised altruism, that is the norm that:

> ... professionals should do everything they can for a client, to a degree even at the expense of maximising their own distinct interests. Correlatively, the norm proscribes professionals acting in the ways that will result to their advantage, and not only

> monetary advantage, when this is at the expense of clients. (Merton, 1982 quoted in Crompton, 1990a).

Clearly this norm is a well-established part of the 'professional ethic' that professionals purvey and equally clearly there are many instances of individual professionals failing to comply with the norm. However, as Crompton points out, the frequent failure of the norm is not sufficient evidence of its non-existence.

Moral regulation at the level of the organisation refers to the socialisation of expert labour within the culture of an organisation. The organisation incorporates expert labour so as to achieve a congruence of goals. Again, Crompton recognises the possibility that there will be instances when organisational reality will be far removed from the organic 'clan' model, but this does not mean that such strategies for regulation are generally ineffective.

These two different patterns of moral regulation of expert labour do not necessarily conflict with one another, although it is clear that they are likely to have different outcomes. Whereas organisational incorporation is likely to stress loyalty to the employing organisation, the ideology of professionalism is likely to engender a wider or more universalistic responsibility. What is less clear is the situation which arises when an expert employee is subjected to both of these patterns, for example as solicitor working for a multi-national company, or a town planner employed by a local authority.

Nevertheless, the view that professionalism is but one mode of regulation of expert labour avoids the pitfalls of the trait approach. It also permits a perception of expert labour, and of those occupations which are generally called professions, which can account for the possibility that these occupations are not solely characterised by self interest. Whilst it is clearly in the interests of those possessing the asset of expertise (however valid or otherwise that might be considered to be) to adopt mechanisms of social closure or professionalisation to protect and further their social and political circumstances, it is also necessary to recognise that such experts and professionals 'do possess cognitive and technical competencies which are important, if not always essential, for the social development of productive forces and the full satisfaction of human needs. By choice and socialisation, they are often deeply involved with the intrinsic value of their calling' (Larson, 1977, p.243).

Professionalisation and the state

Larson argues that the process of professionalisation must be understood as the process through which the producers of special services seek to constitute and control a market for their expertise. It is, therefore an historically specific process which has enabled certain occupational groups to translate one order of scarce resources - that is special knowledge and skills - into another - social and economic rewards (Larson, 1977). However, not all groups have been able to achieve this privileged status, and many aspiring groups fail. The reasons for such failure will vary, but most writers agree that it is clear that the key factor is state support or sponsorship in that professional status is granted either implicitly or explicitly by the state (Johnson, 1972; Friedson, 1973; Larson, 1977; Wilding, 1982).

In order to secure the characteristic advantages associated with professional status - particularly those of the 'elite' professions such as law and medicine - an occupational group needs state support or even sponsorship. The legal protection of professional monopolies, peer group control of professional standards and the power to control entry into the profession are all the direct or indirect consequence of state action, or in Johnson's term, 'mediation' (Johnson, 1972). In the case of the 'welfare professions' such as social work or town planning, the state may be a near monopoly employer and will have effectively sponsored the professionalisation of these occupational groups.

Thus, the relationship which any particular occupational group establishes with the state is a crucial factor in that group's quest for professional status. Wilding argues the symbiotic nature of this relationship:

> The links between the professions and the state are those of interest, class, ideology and mutual dependence. Occupations develop because what they do is useful to someone, or meets a need - genuine or manufactured. Professions evolve for just such reasons, but all depend for their development on state action whether that action be the organisation of services, the provision of finance or the creation of professional monopolies. Equally the state needs professions to fulfil the responsibilities which modern governments assume, to legitimise state power, to make available expertise, to deal with the common situations of industrial society. The state and professions need each other, their functions and powers have grown side by side in an alliance at different times firm and precarious, explicit and implicit. (Wilding, 1982, p.65).

Thus, although the process of professionalisation involves state mediation, the resulting profession is likely to have achieved a degree of autonomy and independent power. The attempts by recent British governments to control and limit professional monopolies have met with only limited success, and in major part this has been due to the entrenched power of the professional institutions who have been able to appeal to popular opinion over the heads of governments and to mobilise support in influential circles. This fact emphasises the position of professionals as members of the dominant class or group within society, with access to wide resources of power and influence. This position not only enables middle class occupational groups to achieve professional status for their occupations, but also permits them to defend those interests against aggression.

Professionalisation centres largely on the claims of an occupational group to control over a particular area of knowledge or expertise. Thus, the main instrument of professional advancement 'is the capacity to claim esoteric and identifiable skills - that is to create and control a cognitive and technical base' (Larson, 1977, p.180). In effect this means credentialisation, which in turn means that professionalism ensures that only the professionals are qualified to judge the quality of this cognitive base and the educational and credentialisation systems which legitimise and support it. However, as Johnson has pointed out, the highest status tends to be achieved by those occupations where the technical content is relatively low and where the element of non-technical interpersonal skills are most important, as in the case of barristers (Johnson, 1977, p.58). Equally, it is probable that as individual professionals' careers unfold, they are likely to spend more time in non-technical managerial activities which have no particular professional specificity.

The importance of credentials in a strategy of professionalisation is clear, since one part of professional ideology is the claim of a direct relationship between the length of professional training and status. High economic and social rewards are justified by the length of time which is required to achieve certain skills. However, Larson claims that professionalism is characterised by overtraining. In part this is an element in a strategy of professionalisation - the need to demonstrate the complexity of the cognitive base and the commensurate need for a lengthy period of training. Equally, however, overtraining 'aims at creating complete skills and at eliciting the layman's trust'. It serves to confer power on the holder of professional credentials because overtraining protects the 'intelligence of the whole', the potential for understanding a whole field and its evolutionary dynamics' (Larson, 1977, p.231). Thus, although professionals may utilise only a small proportion of the knowledge gained during a lengthy period of credentialisation, they gain, through overtraining, the 'intelligence of the whole' which marks them out from other workers. It was precisely this comprehension of the whole process of production that was removed from skilled workers by mechanisation and scientific management (Abercrombie and Urry, 1973).

Professionalism and bureaucracy

The symbiotic nature of the relationship between the professions and the state has been noted above, and although this relationship features strongly in the more recent literature on professionalism, it is the associated, though not synonymous, relationship between professionalism and bureaucracy which is the recurring feature of the earlier literature on the subject. In part the focus on this relationship stems from Parsons' classic distinction between 'professionals' and 'bureaucrats' as occupations characterised by two different types of authority, that is authority derived from expertise as contrasted with authority derived from managerial office (Crompton, 1990b). This position is closely related to the 'trait' approach and as was argued above, this view of professions as occupations is less helpful than one which understands professionalism as a mode of regulation of expert labour. Nevertheless, it is important to recognise the existence of the ideological assertion that professionalism represents a 'free' autonomous and independent form of work organisation, in contrast to, and in conflict with, the restrictive, rational form of bureaucratic organisation. As Scott (1966) argued, professional decisions are too complex and difficult to be controlled through bureaucratic mechanisms. Such decisions require a degree of work autonomy incompatible with bureaucracy. However, this distinction and conflict is more imagined than real. As Larson points out:

> ... in a bureaucratised world, professions can no longer be interpreted as inherently anti-bureaucratic. Both professions and bureaucracy belong to the same historical matrix: they consolidate in the early twentieth century as distinct, but nevertheless complementary modes of work organisation. (Larson, 1977, p.199).

Larson and others (*e..g* Laffin, 1986) argue that professionals are now found predominately within large-scale organisations particularly governmental organisations. This is clearly true of many of the newer, welfare professions, such as social work and town planning, but, argues Larson, it is increasingly true of all professions, reflecting the increasing domination of large-scale commercial organisations and government.

Larson argues that two types of organisational profession may be identified, Firstly, the public service professions - those expert occupational categories which have emerged to service the burgeoning functions of the modern capitalist state, whether those functions are carried out by the state itself or by private or semi-public institutions. Teachers, public health inspectors, social workers, town planners and housing managers all fall within this category. The second category, which Larson calls the techno-bureaucratic professions, encompasses those occupations whose members are responsible for carrying out administrative and managerial functions within both the public and private sectors, for example, hospital administrators, management analysts, business administrators and educational managers.

Larson then, views professions primarily as types of occupation, and as was argued above, this approach is less revealing than one which views professionalism as one mode of moral regulation of expert labour. Nevertheless, in the context of the study of public service professionals in general, and town planners in particular, Larson's division of organisation professionals into categories of public service and techno-bureaucratic serves as a useful heuristic device to assess the ways in which expert labour functions within large organisations. In particular, it would be revealing to see if public service professionals, on achieving promotion tend to rely less upon their technical professional skills and expertise, and more upon skills of a managerial or administrative nature. Thus if they become, in Larson's terms, techno-bureaucratic professionals, they may involve, in Wright's terms a shift in their personal 'assets' from the skill to organisation. Moreover, in Crompton's terms, such a shift may involve a change in the form of moral regulation of expert labour.

Expert labour and bureaucratic power

So far, this chapter has concentrated upon ways in which various occupational groups have been able to exploit their control over, or monopoly of, skills or types of expert labour. Inevitably, this discussion has focused upon professionalism and the process of professionalisation, since these represent the clearest strategies for occupational closure around the resource of expertise or skill. However, it is quite clear that organisations generally, and the bureaucratic form of organisation in particular, provide significant opportunities for certain occupational groups to further and consolidate their own objective interests. Bureaucracies are, of course, but one form of organisation, but they are nevertheless the dominant form of work organisation in capitalist economies, and they are the characteristic form of organisation for the state and governmental agencies. For these reasons, the focus here will be upon the bureaucratic form of organisation, although it is recognised that other forms exist, for example co-operative management or the 'clan' form of organisation characteristic of Japanese corporations (Ouchi, 1979, 1981).

Max Weber saw the bureaucratic form of organisation as an inevitable part of developed capitalist and communist societies. It was the form of organisation and administration most suited to the legal-rational type of legitimate authority, and it was based upon the exercise and control of technical knowledge, the characteristic that makes it specifically rational - in many ways, for Weber, the process of rationality and the drive to bureaucratisation are more or less the same thing. Although Weber's ideal type of bureaucracy refers to all formal organisations, he formulated it mainly with the administrative apparatus of the modern state in mind, and his conceptualisation of the bureaucratic form of organisation has dominated subsequent discussions of bureaucracy that they have in many respects been a debate with the ghost of Weber (*e.g.* Albrow, 1970; Mouzelis, 1975; Page, 1985; Smith, 1988). This debate over the character and scope of bureaucracy and the critique of the Weberian position is not central to this dissertation and has been reviewed elsewhere (*e.g.* Ham & Hill, 1984), but the part of the debate which addresses the question of the power of expert officials in public bureaucracies is of obvious relevance.

That public officials have considerable influence upon public policies is widely accepted. Although the ideology of central and local government in Britain claims a division between technical employed 'servants' who advise, and elected members who decide, the reality is somewhat different largely because of the expertise and experience controlled by the public officials, (Porter, 1965) These power resources combine with what Wright (1978) has called a 'political incapacity of non-bureaucrats' to give public sector bureaucrats a prominent role in the process of policy making. This has enabled observers such as Friend and Jessop (1971) to argue that a distinction should be made between decision-making and decision-taking in local government. The former situation occurs when officials within the bureaucracy restrict the area for decision by elected members, for example by offering a limited range of solutions to a particular problem, or by insisting that particular options or courses of action are technically or financially non-viable. A somewhat similar position is taken by Bachrach and Baratz in their classic study of non-decision making, which refers to "the practice of limiting the scope of actual decision-making to 'safe' issues by manipulating the dominant community values, myths and political institutions and procedures" (Bachrach and Baratz, 1963 p.632) Non decision-making is not 'deciding not to act' or 'deciding not to decide'. Rather it is the mobilisation of bias to ensure that issues do not even become matters for decision.

This influence, or capacity to affect or determine policy or decisions stems in major part from the bureaucrats' control over the resources of specialised knowledge (skill assets). However, it must also stem from resources integral to the organisation itself, rather than from the skill assets owned by individual experts. As Weber pointed out:

> Technical knowledge alone does not guarantee the power of the official. In addition there is the knowledge of concrete facts crucial to his behaviour; knowledge of the service. This is imparted to the official alone through the administrative apparatus. (Weber, 1968).

Thus, in influencing decision-making in the ways indicated above, it seems likely that public servants will draw upon their own expertise (skill assets) and the resources available to them by virtue of their position as employees of the organisation (organisation assets). Examples of this latter category would include access to statistical information such as survey material or Council records; knowledge of bureaucratic procedures both inter- and intra-agency; and awareness of the flexibility inherent in the decision-making and administration exercised by other bureaucrats in their own and external agencies.

Although it is clear that public servants have the capacity to influence or even determine policy decisions, it has also been recognised that the processes of policy implementation may also constitute policy making, and may be equally susceptible to influence by bureaucrats. This point was central to Pressman and Wildavsky's (1973) study of public policy in the United States and has been echoed by several subsequent analysts, for example, Barrett and Fudge (1981), who argue that the distinction between policy and implementation is artificial, and that the policy process should be viewed as a 'policy-action continuum', shaped by a variety of actors at different levels within the organisation.

The important point about this for the purpose of this study is that is raises the possibility that experts in bureaucracies may operate on the decision-making process in different ways, depending upon their position in the bureaucratic hierarchy. This point has been partly explored in the work of Lipsky (1980) and his colleagues (Prottas, 1978,1979) who discuss the role of 'street-level' bureaucrats, those official such as teachers, doctors, policemen and social workers who are in the 'front line' of service provision. Lipsky argues "that the decisions of street-level bureaucrats, the routines they establish, and the devices they invent to cope with uncertainties and work pressures, effectively become the policies they carry out" (1980, p.xii) This position reinforces the views of implementation outlined above. However, Lipsky and his colleagues are also concerned to understand how individuals within bureaucracies seek to bring some order to their lives, and in the process, reshape public policy. As Lipsky points out:

> ... people often enter public employment......with at least some commitment to service. Yet the very nature of this work prevents them from coming close to the ideal conception of their jobs. Large classes or huge caseloads and inadequate resources combine with the uncertainties of method and the unpredictability of clients to defeat their aspirations as service workers. (Lipsky, 1980, quoted in Ham and Hill, 1985).

Thus street-level bureaucrats abandon ideals and adopt mechanisms which enable them to control their work situations and 'manage' clients. They end up 'processing people' in a routinised way. In major part, argues Lipsky, this is because there is no theoretical limit to the demand for free public goods, and therefore welfare services, and those that manage and provide them are always going to be under pressure. Although Lipsky is not seeking to contradict the view that 'experts' can manage and manipulate 'the system' in their own interests, he is suggesting that for experts in the lower echelons of the hierarchy, such manipulation and control may be more a case of developing survival mechanisms rather than achieving or maintaining advantage.

This discussion raises the related point of the potential conflict between authority based upon expertise, and that based upon hierarchy. Ham and Hill conclude that, as far as the detailed parts of an organisation's functions are concerned, expertise resides primarily in the lower ranks of the hierarchy. Moreover, they argue, this explains why there is likely to be conflict between authority based upon expertise and authority based upon hierarchy within bureaucratic organisations. To use Larsons' terminology, it is likely that there will be conflict between techno-bureaucratic professionals and public service professionals, and in term of modes of moral regulation, conflicts between those experiencing 'clan' modes opposed to those regulated by 'professionalism' (Larson, 1977; Crompton, 1990a).

The discussion so far has sought to establish that, in public sector bureaucracies at least, certain bureaucrats, whether they are categorised as 'experts' or not, have the capacity to significantly influence if not control many matters of policy. In the case of street level bureaucrats it may be that the manipulation of policy through implementation is principally a survival technique for the workers concerned. However, in other cases, the questions must be - in whose interests does this manipulation of policy occur? Taking aside questions of corruption or illegal practice, the obvious answer must be that it is likely to be in the interests of the manipulators themselves, the experts, professionals, managers and administrators, and this is the view taken by Gould (1981).

In writing of what he terms the 'salaried middle class', defined as 'those non-manual career hierarchies which we tend to associate with public and private bureaucracies', Gould argues that the SMC have been the major beneficiaries of welfare state policies in Britain as consumers of services, as producers (that is as public sector workers), and in terms of occupational welfare - the pensions, fringe benefits and additional payments associated with SMC jobs. In contrast, argues Gould, neither capital nor labour has benefited from state social welfare policies as much as the SMC. Gould examines education, housing, pensions and health and concludes that in each of these areas of policy, the consumers who benefit most are the members of the SMC, whether they are employed in the public or private sectors. However, argues Gould, welfare bureaucracies are run by as well as for the SMC. He sees the SMC as creating states of dependency and habits of consumption from which they benefit as the managers and providers of services.

Gould's assertion that the SMC constitute a class, with a degree of 'independence, cohesion and power', which operates in its own interests which are distinct from, and sometimes even in conflict with those of capital and labour, is open to debate and will be considered later. What requires emphasis here is his view that the SMC, as members of both public and private bureaucracies, have demonstrated a capacity to 'dominate labour and manipulate the old ruling propertied class' by virtue of their possession of cultural capital - the managerial, professional and scientific knowledge and skills on which society depends.

A somewhat similar view of the influence of expert bureaucrats and managers underlies the 'urban managerialist' thesis initiated by Pahl in the early 1970's (Pahl, 1975). Drawing on the work of Rex and Moore

(1967) and the studies of writers like Davies (1972) and Dennis (1972), Pahl sought to explain differential levels of access to scarce resources and areal inequalities in the city in terms of the values and goals held by the various managers of the 'urban system', such as town planners and housing managers in the public sector, and estate agents and building society managers in the private sector. This approach was in many ways unsatisfactory - for example, it proved difficult to identify any commonality of approach within various groups of managers, and thus any kind of patterning or regularity in 'gate keeping' decisions became impossible to discern. More generally, the approach tended to over-emphasise the resources available to managers, whilst under-estimating the level of discretion that they might have. Nevertheless, this approach, and the various studies of managers that accompanied it, emphasised the enormous potential for influencing policy which lies in the hands of such experts and managers, at whatever point on the 'policy-action continuum' such decisions might be made, and regardless of whether such decision are made in the public or private sectors. Although the managerialist literature is less committed than Gould to the view that bureaucrats and managers as providers of services do so in a way that overwhelmingly furthers their own interests, the clear tenor of the managerialist studies is that discretion and influence is often exercised in favour of established interests, or in the interests of the managers themselves, rather than on behalf of less powerful social groups.

Experts and state policy making

The foregoing discussion of how experts and bureaucrats might influence and determine policy from their position within particular organisations is, of course, only one part of a consideration of how experts can influence state policy. Experts, usually organised professions, can be highly influential in state policy making at the national level by virtue of their privileged access to government - in short they are likely to participate in a corporatist decision-making process.

Corporatism has been revived as a perspective on government and policy formulation during the last two decades following the publication of Schmitter's influential essay *Still the Century of Corporatism?*, in 1974. What has emerged is a new form of corporatism, often referred to as neo-corporatism in order to define it from the earlier pluralist-inspired writings which were coming to be termed 'corporatist' by the early 1970's, but which simply defined this as the regular and close involvement of organised interests with the public bureaucracy and ministers in the formulation of policy, most usually economic policies. As Williamson points out, the term 'corporatism appeared to be used in a manner synonymous with 'incorporation'. (Williamson, 1989).

Schmitter's contribution was to view corporatism in terms of institutional structure rather than as a form of policy making, which had previously been the case. Williamson argues that the central theme of his work is that:

> ... a corporatist system is institutionally structured in a manner that restricts competition and openness among organised interests. This ordered system stands in contrast to the general ethos of the pluralist system where organised interests are in competition with each other, access is open and organisations are internally independent of the state......If pluralism was the competitive market system of pressure group activity, then corporatism was the system of state-licensed monopoly. (Williamson, 1989 p.11).

Although there is inevitability a considerable level of debate within the corporatist literature as to what is the most appropriate definition of the perspective and approach, Grant's definition is representative of the general approach:

> I use the term 'corporatism' (as a shorthand for liberal or neo-corporatism) to refer to a process of interest intermediation which involves the negotiation of policy between state agencies and interest organisations arising from the division of labour in society, where policy agreements are implemented through the collaboration of the interest organisations and their willingness and ability to secure the compliance of their members, (Grant, 1985).

The important term here is 'intermediation' . This implies that the significance of interest organisations is not their capacity to represent their members interests, but their role as intermediaries, between their members and the state. Thus in major part, interest associations are seen to have a regulatory role over their members. They do not simply make demands on the state but they also perform the role of regulating their membership on behalf of the state. This is linked to the idea of 'private interest government' put forward by Streek and Schmitter (1985), who argue that this involves the devolution of public policy functions to private interest associations. In this view, private associations take on the function of regulating parts of economic and social life instead of these functions being undertaken by the state or the market. This process has, of course, been occurring in contemporary Britain under the banner of deregulation.

Most corporatist writing has been concerned to examine corporatist arrangements within the processes of economic policy making or production rather than in the field of welfare. This is because corporatism as a model is only applicable when the state cannot directly intervene through authoritative regulation and allocation, and where it has to depend on others in order to achieve its ends. This notion of dependency is crucial in that it is this which forces the state to enter into corporatist intermediation since it has influence but not control over the behaviour of producers. However, as Williamson points out, the reasons why the state is largely powerless to achieve change against the wishes of producers are all relevant to what he terms 'welfare corporatism' (Williamson, 1989, p.170).

Producers can wield a range of sanctions, such as labour or investment strikes but also a whole range of more minor acts of non-cooperation which can render policies ineffectual. Producers also hold considerable amounts of information which are essential for effective policy formulation and implementation, and since public decisions are likely to involve considerable degrees of judgement in the face of incomplete knowledge and uncertainty, it is almost impossible to determine objectively what is the 'best' decision. Without the cooperation of the producers in the process it is unlikely that the state will be able to implement policies.

In this sense, welfare or organisation professions may be considered as organised interests within the state system in that they are producers of welfare services. The state therefore needs to enter into corporatist intermediation with professional groups in order to achieve its policy objectives, in much the same way as it enters into intermediation with trades unions or employers' groups in the economic sphere. The precondition of this corporate relationship between professions and government is, of course, that the profession must be seen to be able to deliver - to be capable of controlling and regulating its membership in appropriate ways in order to fulfil the agreed policy objectives. As Wilding points out, the leitmotif of the welfare professions is the claim to be able to solve problems within the pattern of existing social and economic relations, and that such problems are:

> ... marginal, technical and susceptible to solution by appropriate prescriptions of modern medicine, or the latest planning, educational or social work orthodoxies. Such scientific judgments immediately announced the professionals as men of judgement and perception and as reliable allies in the task of maintaining the existing social order. (Wilding, 1982, p.63).

The process is obviously two-way. Professional groups are granted a high level of influence on policy matters in their respective areas and, as was noted before, the state legitimises professional knowledge and credentials. In exchange, the professions are expected to participate in achieving policy goals which fit within certain parameters and limits.

However, it is clear that only a small number of individuals are actually involved or are influential in this corporatist process. As Larson points out, 'a profession is always defined by its elites' (Larson, 1977 p.227). Laffin offers two conceptions which are useful here (Laffin, 1986). Firstly, he identifies the 'professional community', which he defines as the leading professionals:

> ... in the forefront of the formation and modification of professional accounts.....(who) often face difficult problems in trying to reconcile the expectations of those within a profession.....The leaders of a profession, then, typically try to manage the emergence of problems, perceptions and definitions within the public policy arena to lead other actors to conceive of the services of the profession as essential in handling certain problems of social significance.....They tend to modify or reinforce their account of professional practice in accordance with their perceptions of the supports offered and the challenges posed by other actors. More specifically, they have to demonstrate both the relevance of and the accredited status of their claims to knowledge and also their normative competence or reliability in carrying out the tasks involved. (Laffin, 1986 p.24).

One important group of actors that the professional community needs to influence and to work with is the 'policy community'. Laffin defines this as:

> ... a relatively small group of participants which has formed to deal with some identifiable class of problems that have or could become the concern of central government. (p.6).

Normally, such a group would include civil servants, politicians with a special interest in these problems, officials from government or semi-government agencies, and representatives from legitimised and 'respectable' interest groups. Policy communities are stable bodies with strict limitations on access and they are characterised by a 'more or less tacit agreement to confine conflict in the interests of joint action'. They are also characterised by agreement on what constitutes relevant and accepted knowledge and information, and purveyors of new knowledge have to persuade community members of its epistemological acceptability. The professions are, of course, an accredited source of wisdom on this latter point.

Although it is not his specific intention to do this, Laffin's categories usefully illustrate how the corporatist process is likely to operate, and how the process of interest intermediation can be played out in practice. His studies of the policy areas of traffic engineering and housing illustrate the importance of the almost symbiotic relationship that can be identified between the policy community, representing the interests of the state, and the professional community.

Organisation assets, skill assets and expert labour

What insights can this review of the relationships between expert labour and power shed on the conceptions of organisation assets and skill assets discussed in the last chapter, and what questions does this discussion raise about the nature and explanatory value of these concepts?

Although the assets of organisation and skill are theoretically distinct, in the case of organisation professionals there seems to be a blurred boundary between the two. It may be extremely difficult to ascertain whether or not any particular individual or group of individuals within an organisation are exploiting their expertise or their organisation assets. Although Larson's division between public service professionals (skill-based) and techno-bureaucratic professions (organisation-based) makes sense, it may be very difficult to judge how this might work out in practice. For example, is a local authority town planner, responsible for the professional work of six or eight other planners, primarily utilising managerial skills or technical expertise? And is he (for it is likely to be a he) exploiting his skills assets in furthering his economic position, or are organisation assets more important here?

In part, the answer to this problem lies in the appreciation that 'experts' within organisations generally have significantly different circumstances depending on their position in the organisational hierarchy. As the literature reviewed above suggests, technical expertise is likely to reside mainly at the lower end of the hierarchy, and that as public service professionals progress up the career ladder it seems likely that they will increasingly utilise more general managerial and interpersonal skills rather than the technical skills which may have warranted their original appointment. Thus, it is likely that all 'experts' do not exploit expertise, and although this point has been made in the context of holders of PhDs driving cabs (Wright, 1985), it may well be that some experts in expert jobs in reality apply very little in the way of technical expertise. This raises the possibility that skills assets, in the context of organisations, may by simply a mechanism for achieving organisation assets. However, what exactly do organisation assets consist of? Does the concept refer principally to the power and authority conferred upon particular individuals or groups of individuals within organisations by virtue of their positions? If this is the case, control of organisation assets may be utilised or exploited to further the interests of a particular class or social group (for example as the consumers of services), and the individual may benefit only in terms of membership of that group or class. Utilising organisational structure to 'empire build' and further personal power and remuneration within the organisation is possible, as is employing a knowledge of organisational structures to effectively achieve career advancement. However, in all of these cases organisation assets are non-transferable and can be very easily lost. One possible exception is that organisation assets may be interpreted as knowledge of organisational procedures and practices, in which case it may be possible for individuals to take this knowledge and sell it on the open market, thus exchanging one asset for another.

The concept of skill assets or cultural capital is equally problematic. As the discussion of professions above indicated, the actual capacity to perform a technical skill may be less important than the capacity of any particular professional organisation to convince the state and the public that the expertise purveyed is important, and complex and the result of an extended period of training. Moreover, since expertise may be understood as a commodity that has been expropriated from others, there are obvious advantages to the credentialed in ensuring that their esoteric knowledge remains inaccessible. Thus, skill assets may be a reflection of social and power relations rather than any particular and precise capacity to achieve particular ends by employing actions derived from a body of theoretical knowledge. It may well be that in the case of organisation professionals, actual technical skills are not as important as they might be to experts operating outside of bureaucratic frameworks, where their technical capacities are regularly exposed to market testing.

The division between the private and public sectors, between organisational professionals and those working in traditional modes and between those who rely primarily on skill as opposed to organisational assets has formed a major part of the current debate on the asset approach to class formation. These cleavages and the more general questions concerning the character and utility of the concept of skill and organisational assets will be further examined in Chapters Four and Five in the context of an examination of the profession and activity of town planning.

Expert labour and town planning

Turning now to the profession and policy area of town planning, what insights can the literature and research reviewed in this chapter offer? Planning is clearly a 'profession' with a Royal Charter, and although it might be possible to mount a discussion as to whether it exhibits the characteristics of a 'full profession' rather than a 'semi-profession' a much more fruitful discussion would centre on the mechanisms for the regulation of the expert labour involved. Are experts in planning subject to the 'professional' mode of regulation, and if so, what form does it take and how does it occur? Or is the 'clan' form more powerful given that the majority of planners are employed by the public sector, and are there identifiable distinctions to be made between the public and private sectors?

The control of land use and development is an activity which has considerable social and economic importance for most societies and it is therefore not surprising to find that the successive British governments have identified planning as an important area of policy, both for the effective operation of a capitalist economy and as a mechanism for achieving certain social and political objectives. Given this situation is therefore to be expected that the occupational group most concerned with this activity, and claiming expertise within this area, has managed to achieve professionalisation fairly quickly. What is less clear is the status and nature of the relationship which exists between the profession of planning and the state, and the degree to which it may be characterised as corporatist. If the professionalisation of planning may be described as a 'corporatist bargain' (Reade, 1987), what tensions may be identified within the profession in normative terms, bearing in mind that 'a profession is always defined by its elites'.

Moreover, does the planning profession tend to exhibit organising or disorganising tendencies in the context of capitalist social relations, or does it exhibit both?

The themes of 'skills' and 'expertise' have run through the chapter, and in some areas of activity there may be little difficulty in defining what these are - in civil engineering or gynaecology for example. However, in the field of town and country planning this expertise may not be so easily pinned down - what exactly is the planners' claimed body of esoteric knowledge which has justified professionalisation? Moreover, if expert knowledge is viewed as a expropriated commodity, and if few readily identifiable technical skills can be demonstrated, the precise historical reasons for professionalisation need examination with a view to assessing the current role of the profession in relation to the requirements of the state.

Finally, if skill assets are viewed as transferable, that is to say they may eventually be exchanged for organisation assets or, more probably, economic assets, would it be reasonable to find some kind of unitary value system within the profession which allocated greater status to the more highly paid members of the profession working in the private sector? Furthermore, how do members of the profession perceive their careers developing? Is there a commitment to public service professionalism and the continued exploitation of skill assets in either the public or private sectors, or can a drive to techno-bureaucracy be discerned as being a more effective road to power, status and financial reward? Bearing in mind that for some planners other sources of finance may be available, from investments, other household incomes, inheritance and so on, these questions of career perceptions, utilisation of assets and normative questions of altruism, service and professional responsibility combine together to create a picture of a profession which may be more complex than that assumed by the literature discussed in this chapter.

These issues relating to profession, expertise and the utilisation of assets in the process of class formation will be explored further in the next two chapters through an examination of the profession and practice of town and country planning in Britain.

4 The profession of planning

The previous two chapters have considered the existing research conclusions and theoretical debates which can inform an understanding of middle class occupational groups, particularly those organizational professions which have secured superior rewards and conditions of employment by virtue of their claim to exclusive cognitive competencies. This chapter and the next examine one such group, Chartered Town Planners, with a view to assessing a series of propositions which form part of the 'asset approach' to the analysis of class formation. In particular, these chapters look at town planners in order to assess how they might utilise assets, particularly the assets of skills, expertise and credentials, in order to secure, maintain and enhance their position. This process of investigation in turn will permit certain conclusions to be drawn about the profession of planning and the work that planners do.

The emphasis here is upon the planners themselves, rather than the process of planning, though as Reade (1987) argues, the profession and the activity of planning are in many respects synonymous. However, it must be recognised that this comment in effect refers, to use Laffin's term, to the 'professional community' rather than the profession or occupational group as a whole. As was pointed out in the last chapter, it is the professional elite, the leaders of the profession, whose views, attitudes and expectations are likely to dominate academic, political, and possibly, popular perceptions of the profession. In contrast, the emphasis in this and the succeeding chapter is more upon the rank-and-file membership of the profession.

The reasons for this are two-fold. Firstly, in order to assess propositions concerning class formation and the utilisation of assets, it is not necessary to focus upon the most senior members of an occupational group. On the contrary, such a focus will inevitably produce unrepresentative findings. Secondly, although a great deal has been written about the planning process and the profession generally, the planners themselves have been largely neglected. Whilst a considerable amount is known about the views of the 'professional community' of planning over a long period of time, the attitudes and values of the rank-and-file have been ignored by academic researchers. In many ways this is a surprising omission since it is quite possible that the views of the professional community may differ considerably from those of the general membership who are undertaking the day to day business of planning. Moreover as will be shown below, conflicts between the leaders and the general membership of the planning profession have occurred before, and there is no reason to suppose that there is, or can be, any kind of professional unanimity spanning the whole of the professional membership. For these reasons alone, in order to gain an understanding of the function and significance of experts in the field of planning, it is necessary to by-pass the pronouncements of the professional community and examine the membership directly. This chapter then, reviews the planning process with a view to understanding the position of 'the planners' within this, as preparation for a review of the survey findings outlined in Chapter Five.

The purpose of planning

In order to understand the role of expert labour in planning it is first necessary to ask 'what is the purpose of planning'? More specifically, what do the planners themselves define as the purpose of planning? For Lewis Keeble, author of the 1950's text book of 'legally-practicable planning', the answer was unproblematic. Planning is:

> the art and science of ordering the use of land and the character and siting of buildings and communication routes so as to secure the maximum practicable degree of economy, convenience and beauty. (Keeble, 1952, P.9).

An uninspiring definition perhaps, and one that does not reflect the "zest and enthusiasm (for planning) of the years immediately after the Second World War" (Mellor, 1977, p.135), but it is one which nevertheless implies a high level of expertise amongst those practitioners who claimed to be able to deliver the physical infrastructure necessary to achieve the brave new world. Moreover, it is a definition which was widely accepted by members of the then rapidly expanding town planning profession, and by politicians and the public. As Hague argues:

> The notion that planning was a neutral and effective means of furthering the interests of everybody was consolidated by the particular political conditions of the 1930's and the war. Rational executive action was a bulwark against the alternatives of laissez-faire and totalitarianism. The economic problems of recession and then reconstruction, and the political problems of refashioning class compromise, strengthened the credibility of an expertise that could manipulate the processes of urban and regional change so as to eliminate dysfunctions (Hague, 1984, P. 101).

In many respects, the immediate post war period represented a peak in the fortunes of the profession and activity of town planning in Britain, a peak which falls in the chronological centre of a history of professionalisation, of government activity and of a social movement which has been bounded by the years of the twentieth century. Some forty-five years after Parliament approved the 1947 Town and Country Planning Act, which effectively established the current system of statutory town planning, the purpose of planning as defined by Keeble is no longer so clear. Moreover, the general support for town planning which most commentators agree existed in the immediate post-war years has largely evaporated (*e.g.* Brindley, 1989; Hardy, 1990). The last twenty years in particular have seen a significant number of criticisms of the planning process and the planning profession, in terms of their failure to achieve much, if not most, of the vision of a new Jerusalem implied in Keeble's view of planning. Planning has been condemned by the political left as having the function of promoting capitalist accumulation (*e.g.* Dear & Scott, 1981); criticised by the right as being inflexible, bureaucratic and restrictive towards enterprise (*e.g.* Ehrman, 1988); attacked by representatives of community organisations as being insensitive and inhuman (*e.g.* Davies, 1972); accused of muddled thinking and 'unreason' (*e.g.* James, 1980) and so on. The catalogue of criticisms from academics, politicians, journalists, community activists, business representatives, industrialists and farmers is endless. If planning emerged as the 'child of consensus' (Thornley, 1991), it is certainly no longer in that happy position.

The reasons for these changes have been extensively described and analysed from a variety of perspectives - see for example Ashworth

(1954); Cherry (1974); Ravetz (1986); Ambrose (1986) and Reade (1987), and it is neither necessary nor appropriate to review this history again here. However, in order to understand the motivations and normative positions of contemporary professional town planners, it is useful to briefly summarise the circumstances which have influenced changing perceptions of the purpose of planning within the profession itself. Furthermore, if the skills and expertise claimed by planners are to be adequately assessed, it is necessary to view them in the context of the aims and purposes that they are directed towards. As will be shown, the planners' expertise is something that has shifted and changed in response to the different interpretations of the purposes of planning as defined by the profession.

Nevertheless, although the planning profession's perceptions of its purpose have altered over time, usually in response to the need to command or retain legitimacy, it is important to recognise that most, if not all of the themes implicit in Keeble's definition still have currency today. Gordon Cherry, one of the most prolific and established writers on town planning and its history, writing in the early 1980's, described the purpose and role of planning in this ambitious statement;

> It deals with the problems of contemporary urbanisation, not only remedying malfunction, but also creating the conditions for harmonious living. (Health, beauty and convenience have long been standing objectives in securing model cities). It deals with the allocation of land for stated purposes; it seeks to relate economic planning to the physical structuring of cities; and it aims to enhance living conditions for the community as a whole (Cherry, 1981, P.4).

It is this naive and unproblematic assumption of the commonality of interests and the capacity of town planning to achieve them that has tended to dominate the planners' perceptions of themselves.

Planning, reform and the 'public interest'

One recurring theme throughout the literature on town planning is the underlying assumption within the profession that planning is uncontroversially in the interests of all. This self-image of planners since the formation of the Town Planning Institute in 1913 has been heavily influenced by an assumption that the purpose of planning is to provide a more rational pattern of land use than that determined by the market, and that this pattern will unquestionably be in 'the public interest'.In part, this claim to altruism is to be expected from an occupational group seeking to professionalise. However, in planning, the assertion that the purpose of planners and the planning process is to provide a future which will be of benefit to all is a belief which is integral to the practice of the activity of planning, in a way that a claim to altruism by say, dentists, doctors or engineers is not.

In part, this naive assumption about the purpose of planning stems from the writings and achievements of the 'founding fathers' of the town planning movement, in particular Ebenezer Howard, Patrick Geddes and Raymond Unwin. Whilst there were undoubtedly significant differences of approach and belief between these three - for example Howard had been substantially influenced by Utopian Socialism and Communitarianism, whilst Geddes, the biologist, was altogether a much more conservative man - a reading of the voluminous literature on these influential figures and the other early planners (for example Thomas Adams, Patrick Abercrombie, George Peplar and Thomas Sharp) reveals a widespread commitment to planning as a 'science and art' to benefit all (Cherry, 1974; 1981).

In his review of the 'ideology of planning' Davies (1972) catalogues the attitudes of successive members of the 'professional community' of planners during the first sixty years of this century, emphasising the perception of 'planning' as being synonymous with 'public interest'. However, he also quite correctly illustrates the corollary of this, that is the assumption that planners know best; that they alone have the vision of what the future can and should be like and that their task is to pursue this vision, overriding the limited and misguided views of politicians, property owners and the public. On the basis of his study of the planning of Rye Hill in Newcastle, Davies argues that planners have taken on the mantle of 'Evangelistic Bureaucrats':

> in order to immunise themselves to the persistent criticism made of them as they exercise their trade ..... If this type of official legitimates his schemes not by reference to the actual consumer, but either in terms of his own self-proclaimed and self-induced charisma or by reference to the range of putative consumers whose wishes and wants he himself can, in impunity define, then how can we deny or control him? The discourse of democracy is vitiated, and we the citizens are forced to give up more and more of the areas of decision-making to a group of powerful, highly trained officials possessing, it would appear, a range of quasi-magical potencies (Davies, 1972 p.3).

This view of the purpose of planning ascribed to planners raises two further, related, issues. The first of these is the significance of rationality, the second, the linked assumption that planning is a progressive activity. Some thirty years ago Reissman pointed out that the town planning movement had an organising myth, that of 'reason'. The planners believed that "man is rational. He can plan, and thereby create a better more harmonious and more humane environment for himself" (Reissman, 1964 p.45).

Twenty years later, Cooke emphasised the significance of rationality for planning again:

> ... it has been proposed that urban and regional planners operated according to a broad set of shared assumptions about the spatial development process in the post-war years. The consensus may be plainly stated as one in which it was assumed that rational intervention by an educated elite could produce modifications to the development process which would improve the welfare of all members of society. It was further assumed that there were no serious disagreements between the main social groupings in liberal democracies, all sharing the belief that there were substantial welfare gains to be achieved from social democratic planning (Cooke, 1983 p.87).

These pluralist assumptions are closely associated with the belief that the process of planning is progressive, in that it somehow achieves an improvement in the circumstances and living conditions of the 'less-well-off'. This in part stems from the assertion that town planning as an activity of government was a direct consequence of the 'sanitary reforms' of the mid- to late-nineteenth century. This assertion is frequently made in the planning literature. For example, Cullingworth's standard text on town planning in Britain clearly states in the first line of the book that town planning developed from public health and housing policy. He goes on to argue that the first piece of town planning legislation, the Housing, Town Planning, *etc.*, Act of 1909, was essentially an extension of sanitary policy. Given the general acceptance that sanitary reform constituted an improvement in the living standards of the labouring classes in the late nineteenth and early twentieth centuries, town planning could therefore, by association also be considered 'progressive'. This view was undoubtedly reinforced by the association of planning with the passing of the post-Second World War package of legislation that came to be regarded as the foundations of the welfare state.

However, as several commentators have pointed out, the perception of these important pieces of town planning legislation as being somehow progressive or reformist is mistaken. McDougall (1979) shows that the 1909 Housing and Town Planning Act was passed to resolve conflicts between particular fractions of capital, rather than to achieve 'reform' for the working class. As she points out, there is no evidence of a labour movement demand for town planning legislation, and "it would be naive to see any piece of social legislation or policy as the spontaneous expression of benevolence on the part of the state or its agencies" (p.378).

McDougall argues that the 1909 Act must be seen as an attack by industrial and commercial capital upon landed interests:

> For the land clauses in the Town Planning Act and the Finance Bill were intended to destroy the remaining economic advantages attached to land ownership, thus eroding the economic basis of the landowners' social and political position. These clauses were particularly aimed at preventing landowners from benefitting from the development activities of industrial, commercial and public capital in urban areas. Furthermore, the town planning legislation, by allowing a local authority to prepare schemes for adjacent land, enabled municipal authorities, for the first time, to control their suburban development and expansion ... The balance of power was shifted from the County Councils, dominated as they were by landowning interest, to municipal authorities dominated by the interests of industrial and commercial capital (McDougall, 1979, p.378).

A somewhat similar position is taken by Backwell and Dickens in their review of the 1947 planning legislation (Backwell and Dickens, 1978). They argue that the policies contained in the 1947 Act may only be understood in the context of the balance of power firstly between the different fractions of capital and secondly between capital and labour. The effect of the war was to enhance the position of labour vis-a-vis capital, due to high levels of employment; to advantage industrial capital at the expense of rural landed interests; and to temporarily place finance capital at a disadvantage, although in the long term to provide massive opportunities for property development through post-war reconstruction. Backwell and Dickens argue that the 1947 planning legislation, passed by a 'pioneering' Labour government, had been largely determined by a handful of influential individuals (who were mainly conservative) in the early 1940's.

Thus, the legislation was a reflection of the pre-war and wartime governmental reports of Barlow (Royal Commission on the Distribution of the Industrial Population, 1940), Uthwatt (Committee on Compensation and Betterment, 1941), and Scott (Committee on Land Utilisation in Rural Areas, 1942). The conclusions of these reports and their recommendations, argue Backwell and Dickens, are a reflection of the conflicts between fractions of capital and between capital and labour, and cannot be simply understood as reforms designed to improve the living circumstances of the working class, even if such reforms may help in securing the 'mass loyalty' of the populace during time of war. As McDougall emphasises:

> Any social legislation is the product of a particular social and economic system, the product of a particular configuration of class demands and interests. To view a piece of legislation or policy as autonomous from this structure, as say the result of an impartial desire to eradicate social problems or the influence of philanthropists or the writings of social reformers, is to ignore the history of social policy in this country. Particular pieces of legislation inevitably reflect the interests and values of those with power and influence and their attempts to deal with the class demands which confront them (McDougall, 1979, p.375).

Despite evidence and arguments such as those described above, it is still common to find statements in the professional planning press, such as *The Planner* (the official journal of the Royal Town Planning Institute), which continue to imply that planning is a reformist and progressive activity. Reade (1987) argues that in part this is because planners are extraordinarily reluctant to be 'backward looking'. By this he means there has been a reluctance to undertake evaluative studies of the outcomes of planning policies and decisions. The emphasis has always been on the future, rather than the past, and this has prevented planners from coming to terms with the possibility that the consequences of their actions might be regressive rather than progressive. Reade points out that very few evaluative studies of past planning decisions have been carried out, and those that have, most notably Peter Hall's *The Containment of Urban England* have concluded that the principal beneficiaries of planning decisions and actions are invariably the property-owning middle classes, 'commercial and industrial interests' or landowners. The 'working class', council tenants and inner city residents are categories who without exception are judged to have failed to benefit from planning. The conclusions of

Simmie's study of Oxford (Simmie, 1981) and Hague's examination of Edinburgh (Hague, 1984) confirm Hall's findings.

All of the above leads Reade, in his comprehensive and critical review of British town and country planning, to conclude that the planning profession still operates at the evangelical level of what he terms 'belief' rather than at the level of a search for knowledge (Reade, 1987, p.157):

> 'Belief' describes the situation in which the politicians and the public entrust decision making largely to the professional and experts who staff the public bureaucracies, and in which those professionals and experts themselves also possess a considerable measure of belief in their own capacity to find the best solution; the belief is two-sided. The reason why so much is entrusted to these elites is that these are the people whom, we might say, 'society' has duly authorised as competent within their given subject areas. The credibility of the solutions they arrive at, therefore, and the reason why these solutions are themselves accorded 'belief', lies in the accredited competence of the advisers concerned, more than in the intellectual credibility of the solution which they propose (Reade, 1987, p.96).

Given the above assessment, it was perhaps not surprising to find a recent (1990-1991) President of the Royal Town Planning Institute taking as the theme for his presidential year the slogan 'Believing in Planning'. In effect, this was an evangelical exhortation to Institute members to commit themselves to the kind of assertions and assumptions embodied in the 'founding fathers' view of planning as an uncontroversially 'good' activity, which must benefit all. The fact that this President was widely viewed as a 'radical', and was a member of the Institute's Radical Institute Group, a loose coalition of members committed to left of centre policies, indicates the pervasive nature of Reade's 'belief', at least within the 'professional community' of planning. The existence of deep social, economic and political divides within society, of deep differences of values and beliefs, of varied and conflicting views as to what might constitute the 'public interest' are sociological axioms which the professional community and much of the membership of the profession of planning have tended to ignore.

The planning profession and internal conflict

The apparently widespread acceptance within the profession of the view that 'planning' equates with 'public interest' seems to imply an occupational group exhibiting a high level of homogeneity and a clear perception of its role and purpose, however naive and misguided that might be. On the contrary, however, planning both as an activity and a profession has been dogged by a number of irreconcilable conflicts which have in turn determined much of its character, and which have been the focus for much internal dispute and wrangling within the profession. Moreover, these conflicts may be seen as the source of much of the confusion, ambiguity and vagueness which characterises many of the profession's public pronouncements. These conflicts may be summarised as firstly, between planning's role as an activity of government and the legacy of its role as a social movement bequeathed by the 'founding fathers'; secondly, between planning as provider of social goods whilst at the same time meeting the needs of the market; and thirdly, between the planner's role as a 'professional' and that of a 'bureaucrat'.

The origins of town planning in Britain were those of a pressure group. The Garden City Association (later the Town and Country Planning Association) was founded in 1899 to pursue Ebenezer Howard's ideas for the construction of new free-standing settlements away from existing urban areas. As Hague (1984) notes, by the time of the passing of the 1909 Housing and Planning Act, there were only four men practising as professional planners. In these early years of the twentieth century, the town planning movement:

> ... was a small pressure group, drawing support from the professions (principally architects, surveyors and engineers, the three bodies who supported the foundation of the Town Planning Institute in 1913), with little mass support. Its closest connections were with other groups such as the Fabians, the Sociological Society and the National Housing Reform Council. All these sought to provide ideas for 'men of influence', and remained remote from the violent social upheavals of the period before and after the First World War, (Mellor, 1977, p.127).

However, as Gordon Cherry, the official historian of the Town Planning Institute has noted , by 1939 the town planner had become less of a dedicated reformer and more of an officer of local government (Cherry, 1974, p.117).

The development of town planning during the post-war period was as an activity of the state, and throughout the second half of this century, the overwhelming majority of planners, around 80%, have been employed as public servants:

> Planning has increasingly become that which is legally practicable, rather than a strategy for the reconstruction of society, but it still retains the Utopian quality of its early days, (Mellor, 1977, p.136).

The nature of the conflict generated by this situation is obvious. On the one hand, planners must see themselves as employees of the state required to fulfil the needs and demands of managing land use within a capitalist economy, whilst on the other, the collective conscience of the profession implies a capacity to instigate real reform through the manipulation of the physical environment - planning as an article of faith (Cherry, 1991). Disregarding the question marks over the viability of this latter position, the existence of these two conflicting situations has tended to generate a confusion of purpose within the profession generally and within the professional community in particular.

The second area of conflict is related but distinct and is often referred to as the market/intervention contradiction. As Thornley (1990) points out, this market/intervention contradiction is mentioned by a number of writers (*e.g.* Broadbent, 1977; Ravetz, 1980; Reade, 1987), and it refers to the conflict which exists in the work of planners when they on the one hand co-operate with the private sector in order to secure conditions necessary for investment or development, whilst on the other hand they are charged with the political (and professional) objective of planning in the 'public interest'. As Reade and others (*e.g.* Hall, 1989) have pointed out, there is an inherent contradiction here which cannot be resolved without the re-introduction of a system to recoup development value to the state, as was attempted by Labour Governments, and subsequently repealed by Conservative Governments, at various times during the post-war period (1947, 1967 & 1976). This conflict which exists in the day-to-day work of many if not most professional planners has in turn created confusion in the profession as to what might be the legitimate purpose of planning.

The final area of conflict has been referred to in the previous chapter, in that it is the professional/bureaucratic conflict which many public sector welfare professions experience. As Salaman points out, although professions are eager to express their alienation from, and their dissatisfaction with, bureaucratic controls and objectives, professions in bureaucracies tend to 'toe the line' (Salaman, 1979, p.138). This is undoubtedly true of planning, but there is another conflict that has proved more problematic. In the case of planning, there is a confusion as to 'who is the client?' or 'to whom does the planner feel accountable for decisions?'. There are, of course a number of possible answers - the politicians or elected members; the electorate (of the particular local authority); the public (a wider notion to incorporate for example those who work in an area but do not vote); the residents (of the particular area being planned); and so on. Other answers which might be more difficult to adjudicate could include 'myself' or, reflecting the particular ideological circumstances of planning, 'future generations'. Although the conflict is not unique to planning, it is probably more acute than for other occupations, and clearly presents major difficulties and divergences of approach to the purpose of planning.

This has been further compounded by the increasingly high profile played by planners in the private sector over the last decade. Although private sector planners might experience some of the difficulties described in the previous paragraph, their client is usually well-defined, since it is normally the person or organisation paying the professional fees. This shift to the private sector (which will be discussed further below) has had considerable ideological impact upon the profession in recent years. Apart from the attraction of higher salaries, and the removal of much burdensome bureaucracy and obstreperous councillors, a shift from the public sector to the private sector provides the individual planner with a much clearer, and less troublesome, brief in terms of 'purpose'. It is evident that this has not gone unnoticed in the profession at large, and it is clear that the professional journals have given a much more favourable press to private sector planners during the last decade, whereas previously, it had been considered somewhat dubious to act on behalf of a client (usually a landowner or developer) instead of representing the 'public interest' via state employment.

These conflicts, inherent in the profession and practice of planning in Britain today, have played their part in several substantial debates conducted within the RTPI over the purpose of planning and the role that the Institute should play within this. The most notable of these occurred in 1964/5 and 1971. In the first case, the 'professional community' of planning sought the approval of the membership to certain changes liberalising entry to the profession. The thinking behind this was that the character of the profession was changing and that the planner was increasingly operating as part of a team of skills, and no longer as the 'supreme designer'. The proposals generated a palace revolution against the leadership of the Institute, and a clear rejection by the membership of the proposals. In part this was, of course, a reflection of a fear amongst the membership that a liberalisation of entry to the profession would jeopardise status and career prospects. However, it was also a conflict between members of the professional community who had significantly different perceptions about the nature and purposes of planning, rooted in the discussions outlined earlier.

In 1971 the RTPI published a discussion paper which invited members to vote on five possible futures for the Institute. These were:

i no change;

ii a learned society rather than a profession;

iii an Institute of Planning which would embrace all types of planning (corporate, economic, social, environmental);

iv an Institute of Community Planning; and,

v an Institute of Environmental Planning.

The membership voted clearly for the last option, and as Hague points out:

> The final choice of the members thus amounted to an endorsement of the proposition rejected in the 1960's. The scope of planning was broadened slightly, while re-emphasising its professional basis. The very fact that the Institute could credibly consider such a diversity of self-definitions testifies to the uncertainties about its own identity which planners were experiencing, (Hague, 1984, p.111).

In 1976, the Institute published a further pamphlet, 'Planning and the Future' which again considered the different ways in which the profession might change and develop. However, during the last fifteen years the professional community has been less prepared to enter into these kinds of navel-contemplating debates which have tended only to create conflict and controversy, and which have portrayed the profession in a less than positive light.

Planning and the process of professionalisation

In the last chapter, professionalisation was defined as the process through which the producers of special services seek to constitute and control a market for their expertise, while professionalism, following Crompton, was viewed as a form of moral regulation. How do these conceptions fit the occupational group and activity of town planning?

The process of professionalisation began with the formation of the Town Planning Institute in 1913, as a body representing the interest of like minded men. (As Hague (1984) points out, women were not admitted to professional membership of the TPI until 1928). These men, principally from the construction occupations and the law, saw themselves as professionals, and the Institute as the vehicle for defining the nature and skills of the planning activity. More importantly, the founding of the Institute represented the failure of any one of the existing, well-established professional groups to establish legitimate control over this newly emerging area.

Hague describes the claims laid by the engineers, the surveyors and principally the architects, to town planning knowledge, expertise and competence. The engineers, well established as a local government profession, already had a Town Planning Committee. The surveyors, who had both a local government and a private sector role also saw a role for themselves. The Architects, established in 1834 had been dominant in lobbying for the 1909 Act and regarded town planning as their own preserve. They organised an extravagant international Town Planning Conference in 1910 with a glittering guest list including the King, the Archbishop of Canterbury, the Maharajah of Baroda and even Lord Kitchener of Khartoum:

> The town is too precious to be entrusted to the consideration only of its expert surveyors and engineers. The problems are architectural and will be ultimately judged as such, (Address by Beresford Pike to the 1910 conference quoted by Cherry, 1974, p.46).

However, the architects, engineers, lawyers, public health officials, municipal councillors and the few professional town planners who came together in 1913 argued the necessity of an independent Institute, and by implication, an independent profession. In large part this was made possible by the unwillingness of any of the existing professions to cede responsibility for planning to another.

Once established, the Town Planning Institute was careful to keep its distance from the Garden Cities and Town Planning Association, which it considered as militant, 'political' and propagandist (Ravetz, 1986; Reade, 1987). For its own part, the TPI sought to establish itself as technical and non-political - in short it pursued the classic strategies of professionalisation from its inception. By 1920 an examination system had been developed to restrict entry into the Institute, and the first University Department of Town Planning and Civic Design had been created at the University of Liverpool. 'Planning' began to be established as a legitimate, independent and technical activity, distinct from the existing professions. Reade offers a critical view of this process:

> Above all, perhaps, there was the Town Planning Institute, carefully avoiding committing itself to any identifiable cause, maintaining that town and country planning was technical and non-political, and yet itself very much engaged in the highly political task of trying to invent a new profession, with a distinctive and defined sphere of competence. (Reade, 1987, p.45).

With the establishment of a statutory system of town planning in 1947, covering the whole of the country, involving plan preparation and development control, and the passing of legislation to implement the new town programmes in 1946 and the national parks in 1949, the professionalisation of planning was assured. Not only did this legislation require local authorities to undertake planning functions (and thus employ planners), by altering the relationship between public and private rights in development in favour of the former, the legislation also created new tasks for private developers who increasingly needed professional advice (Healey, 1985).

Having established this comprehensive system of land use planning, the government needed to make sure that it could be staffed. In 1948, the Minster for Town and Country Planning, Lewis Silkin, set up the Schuster Committee to enquire into the qualifications of town planners, his concern being to ensure a supply of experts to operate the system, and to widen the disciplinary backgrounds from which they were drawn. The Schuster report was published in 1950, and it argued firmly for more planners with backgrounds in public administration and social science, and for the marriage of architectural and development management expertise with social scientific knowledge.

In its evidence to the Schuster Committee, the Town Planning Institute strongly opposed these arguments, opting instead for a view of planning that emphasised town design, a process best undertaken not by a team of experts, but by 'planners', members of a distinct profession with unique skills. Inevitably, the Institute largely ignored the conclusions of the Schuster Committee, instead encouraging the development of undergraduate and part-time education in 'planning' as defined by the Institute. Healey argues that:

> ... this must be seen as a move by local government personnel to wrest control of planning work from the architecture and engineering consultancies which provided the expertise for much of the immediate post-war planning effort, (Healey, 1985, p.497).

Although the years since 1947 have seen booms and slumps in the fortunes of town planning generally, and the profession in particular, the numbers of Chartered Town Planners have increased from approximately 800 in 1939 to 12,000 in 1991. The profession has been awarded a Royal Charter, and the existence of statutory obligations upon local authorities to maintain planning control and plan making functions has ensured a steady flow of employment opportunities for planners in both the private and public sectors. Despite the alleged 'attacks' on planning undertaken by the Thatcher governments of the 1980's (Brindley, 1989; Thornley, 1991), the planning profession has emerged relatively unscathed, partly because of the difficulties in dismantling a system of planning control which does so much to maintain environmental quality for the middle classes and secures the profitability of the development industry by ensuring scarcity and windfall increases in land value.

In contrast with many other occupational groups, planning achieved professional status rapidly, largely due, of course to the passing of the 1947 Act. Ruth Glass has argued that town planning achieved respectability too easily and too soon (Glass, 1973 p.52), and a somewhat similar point is made by Foley (1960). Both writers argued that professionalisation had been secured before a sound theoretical base for action had been developed. This point will be returned to below, but it is important to note that this lack of a coherent theoretical perspective is a criticism of planning made by many writers (eg Davies 1972; Bailey 1975; Ravetz, 1986, and most notably, Reade, 1987), and one which is significant in the context of professionalisation, in that this process usually involves identifying a body of esoteric knowledge to which the profession lays exclusive claim. Planning somehow managed to avoid doing this in any precise way, the main intellectual energy of planning going into establishing its legal and administrative framework.

In part, the achievement of professional status without declaring a theoretical hand may be seen as a consequence of the rapid development of a planning system in the post-war years. The widespread acceptance of planning as a 'good thing', albeit short lived enabled the profession to assert its technical competence in a largely uncritical climate. Moreover, planning was developing during the 'long boom', a time of expansion and economic growth, when it was possible to imply that the process could meet the demands of all sections of the populations. Under these circumstances, the need to demonstrate a theoretical base for decision making or expertise was less than pressing. Reade, however, argues that the reluctance to specify the intellectual underpinnings of planning was itself part of the strategy of professionalisation. In his view, the legitimation of planning may be seen as a consequence of a strategy which involved an ideology with four components, which he defines as 'physicalism', 'holism', 'technicism', and 'role-confusion'. These interlinked strands were used by the occupation of planning to assist in its search for professional status in order to promote the idea that planning is non-controversial and has a technical imperative.

Physicalism refers to a set of vague ideas which emphasise the importance of the physical environment. Partly, this is a commitment to physical determinism -the belief that changes to the environment can improve human welfare, reduce social problems or induce a sense of community, and partly it is the assertion of the primacy of the natural and built environments as ends in themselves. In any event, the vagueness of the assertions permit planning to appeal to a wide set of interests and opinions.

Holism has similar characteristics in that this set of, again vague, ideas asserts that planning is all-embracing and comprehensive, and that it provides benefits for all interest groups in society. This doctrine says Reade, has enabled planning to enlist support from an amazingly wide range of interest groups. By the same token, holism implies that not only is planning based upon a comprehensive understanding, it is also the vehicle through which conflicts can be resolved.

Technicism is the set of vague ideas which portray planning as technical and somehow objective and 'beyond' politics, even to the extent of scientising planning, which happened most dramatically in the 1960s and early 1970s. Finally, role-confusion describes the tendency of the planning profession to define its tasks broadly or narrowly as seems expedient. When governments have been willing to adopt planning strategies in the social and economic spheres, planners have tended to portray themselves as concerned with a wide range of policy issues. In contrast, under more recent Conservative governments, planning has been much more narrowly defined as a matter of land use and statutory responsibilities, Reade concludes:

> All of the above four strands of planning thought are vague. In order to make their ideas politically acceptable, planners have portrayed planning as non-controversial, and as no more than an obviously and objectively necessary technical response to the problems of a supposedly increasingly 'complex' society, while at the same time contriving to be extremely vague as to what planning does and does not concern itself with. Planning, we might say, has made itself all things to all men. (Reade, 1987 p.35).

Thus, although the process of professionalisation of planning has been similar to that of most professional groups, planning is distinguished by the short length of time taken to achieve professional status and by the reluctance shown by the profession to unambiguously declare its cognitive base. In contrast, planning fits well the model described in the last chapter, where it was argued that professionalisation will only occur if state sponsorship or support is forthcoming, and clearly this was and still is the case with planning. This aspect of the process of professionalisation will be considered a little more under the discussion of professionalism below.

Professionalism and town planning

The conception of professionalism as a mode of regulating expert labour can be readily applied to town planning. The granting of professional status to planners may be seen as a necessary part of managing land and development within a capitalist economy. Reade refers to this as 'the corporatist bargain', by which he means that:

> in exchange for portraying the existing social, political and economic arrangements as reasonably fair and equitable and as therefore legitimate, professions such as teaching, social work and town planning are given a modicum of perceived power and status. In the particular case of town planners, this means that in exchange for economic security and an official definition of their role as 'important', the planners are expected to create the impression that the property industry is regulated, that the worst of its potentially anti-social excesses are kept in check and that all

> land is put to its socially best use, rather than that which maximises private profit or promotes sectional interest, (Reade, 1987, p.132).

It is undoubtedly true that the Institute, throughout its nearly eighty year history, has always sought to portray itself as 'reasonable', 'rational' and non-political. Moreover, like most other professionalising occupations, it has always implied that the problems that its members seek to solve are ultimately resolvable within the existing social and economic structures of society. Although questions such as 'inner city decay' or the problems of de-industrialisation are widely perceived by planners as part of their agenda for action, the approaches to these problems, and the solutions proposed are invariably set within the constraint of capitalist social relations. This is to be expected in the case of policy recommendations made in the context of local government, but there has also been a noticeable reluctance to air views and opinions within the Institute's weekly journal *The Planner* which are in any substantial way critical of government policy or the status quo. A good example of this is the way in which Eric Reade's comprehensive and highly critical appraisal of town planning was largely ignored by the Institute when it was published in 1987. *The Planner* published one review (which indicated the reviewer's almost complete incomprehension of the book's arguments) and in a subsequent issue, Reade was afforded a right of reply. Instead of stimulating a debate, the publication of a major work with the title *British Town and Country Planning* (whatever one might think of the validity of its conclusions), raised hardly a comment in the professional press or within the study groups and forums of the Institute. In contrast, books around the same time which have been more to the taste of the profession, such as Elson's study of green belts (1986) or Peter Hall's *London's 2001* (1989), have received wide consideration and approval.

A more significant instance of this tendency to evade substantial political questions which are integral to the business of land and development, is the question of the taxation or recoupment of development value, sometimes termed 'betterment'. The Uthwatt Report of 1942 made a clear recommendation that a system of planning and the control of development would need to incorporate mechanisms for recouping the increases in land value occurring as a consequence of planning decisions. Consequently, the 1947 Act not only nationalised development rights, it also nationalised development value, and owners who were given permission to develop their land were obliged to pay a development charge amounting to 100% of the difference between the existing use value of the land and its value after the granting of planning permission. This part of the legislation inevitably proved to be unpopular amongst land owners and developers, and the development charge was characterised as a development tax (which it was not) and was eventually repealed by the succeeding Conservative government. Subsequent attempts to introduce similar schemes in 1967 and 1976 were similarly repealed by Conservative administrations.

The 1947 Act thus established a clear link between planning and land value, the importance and significance of which has been widely discussed (*e.g.* Cullingworth, 1980; Ball, 1983; Ambrose, 1986; Reade 1987) and does not need repetition here. What does need to be emphasised is the planning profession's reluctance to address this vital question. The repeal of the 'betterment' clauses of the 1947 Act effectively rendered the planning system toothless, depriving it of income and considerable power. Planning was to become a process driven by the needs of the market rather than a mechanism for ensuring the 'best possible pattern of land use for the community'. In the light of this, the profession's silence on this most major matter is almost beyond belief, and it can only be explained by reference to the profession's deep-seated desire to abstain from any matter of political significance, and to a reluctance to incur displeasure from powerful vested interests.

The last decade has seen the planning profession withdraw from many of the ambitious claims of the late 1960's and 1970's, when planning tended to portray itself as the profession which could oversee and co-ordinate the work of experts, and when the planners' skills were often claimed to be those of 'planning' in the abstract, rather than relating to development and the built environment alone. During the 1980's the emphasis has been more upon a profession which claims a semi-judicial skill in the operation and manipulation of the town and country planning procedures and legislation. This position has enabled planners to move even further away from contentious political issues and from the profession's reforming origins. The last five years has seen an almost total absence of articles in *The Planner* dealing with issues of social reform or social 'problems'. In contrast, there has been an increased interest in these pages with procedural matters and with design and construction concerns such as facing materials for buildings, or brick types.

The last ten years has also seen a major change in the organisation of professional work in that private sector consultancy and development industry work has grown in quantity. Planners have begun to realise that they have an expertise which can be marketed beyond the traditional areas of local and central government and this has had a number of consequences for professional ideas and practice. The first and most obvious of these has been the realization that planning can be personally lucrative. During the mid and latter parts of the 1980s a comparatively small number of planners began to secure earnings and life styles which were considerably superior to those normally associated with state employment. Some of these planners had spent the bulk of their professional careers in private practice, but mechanisms for shedding labour from central and local government, such as early retirement and voluntary severance schemes have encouraged many former local government planners in particular to take their expertise into the private sector. In addition, during the development boom of the mid to late 1980s, many development companies and consultancies recruited experienced planners from local government.

The overall effect of this process has been to loosen the association within the profession between the activity of planning and the notion of 'public service', however that might be defined. This has in turn been compounded by the policies of privatisation and 'contracting out' encouraged by the Thatcher administrations. Planning has not been exempt from this process, and a proportion of the work traditionally undertaken directly by local authority-employed planners is now contracted out to planning consultants. Initially contracted-out work was limited to the preparation of individual research projects or reports, but this has extended to the preparation of appeal statements and local plans, and there are now instances of the whole of a local authority development control function being undertaken by private companies.

These changes raise the possibility of a substantial shift of the professional work force from the public to the private sector, in a manner somewhat similar to surveying. Public agencies therefore become 'clients', and many of the conflicts of purpose endemic to planning which were described earlier in this chapter largely evaporate. Moreover, this potential shift in the character of the profession from what might be described as a 'welfare base' (i.e. serving the 'public interest') to a 'skill base' (selling a skill, expertise or service on the open market), may over time generate changes in the overall character and assumptions of the profession.

It is likely that most people who join the Royal Town Planning Institute do so primarily because of the enhanced career opportunities that membership brings. Although it is quite possible for non-members to practice as planners in the private sector, or to become employed by local authorities, since there is no legal restriction on non-members practising as town planners, they cannot designate themselves as 'Chartered' and they are likely to find that professional membership is widely seen as a necessary credential. This is, of course, testament to the effective lobbying of the Institute, and it is indicative of the wide influence that it has in the field. As the discussion above has shown, it is clear that the Institute does actively regulate the activities and expectations of the profession, and that this is done in a direction and manner which is generally supportive of existing, that is capitalist social relations. Discussions and debates which threaten these relations are discouraged or excluded.

The moral regulation of expert labour in planning can therefore be seen to occur principally through the activities of the Royal Town Planning Institute. Through its weekly journal, mailed to all members; through its annual conference and Summer School (the proceedings of which are again distributed to all members); through the educational requirements placed upon institutions of higher education which offer 'recognised' planning courses; through the publication of a regularly amended code of professional conduct; through the publication and distribution to every member of a series of Practice Advice Notes which seek to regulate professional behaviour in a wide variety of situations; through the activities of its network of regional branches (again in contact with every member) - these are some of the ways in which the professional community of planning defines the legitimate terms of reference and action for its membership.

Given the highly credentialed character of the Institute's membership, it would be naive to assume that these channels constitute a form of professional 'indoctrination'. Clearly, many members will be receptive to these ideas and values, which may have been part of their reason for originally joining the Institute. The importance of these channels seems to be less one of indoctrination and more one of regulation through setting out the 'ground rules' for participation in the process and profession of town planning. In this sense, the profession may be understood as a mode of regulation of expert labour. However, given that most planners work within large organizations, the 'clan' form of regulation may also be important, though given the comments above concerning the changing public/private sector split, it is possible that the clan form may prove to be less significant in the future. It is worth noting that the profession has never been able to exercise 'quality control' over the way in which planning expertise is delivered. In large part this is due to the difficulty in specifying measures of quality control in relation to planning knowledge. However, it is also due to the fact that most planners work in local government and have therefore been subjected to control of their expertise through formal organisational mechanisms, in other words, the clan form of regulation. The next chapter will seek to examine these questions in more details.

Expertise and cognitive competence in planning

What particular skills and forms of expertise do planners possess? As has been indicated above, many writers have been critical of the planners' claim to expert status because they have been unable to demonstrate that their skill and expertise rest upon sound theoretical foundations. Davies (1972) argued that:

> The insubstantial nature of planning utterances is in large measure the consequence of the fact that in many of the subjects (and they are legion) on which planners pronounce there is simply no such thing as an objective body of knowledge allied to a coherent theory which can be used for rational decision-making (Davies 1972. p.222).

Eric Reade forcefully makes a similar point:

> ... it seems likely that in many cases, or to a large extent, it is not planning which determines the pattern of development at all, but that on the contrary it is the market... If, however, the market were in fact to be rendered largely inoperative, as would have occurred if the 1947 Act's 100% recoupment of betterment had continued in force... we would then be brought up sharply against what is probably the central intellectual weakness of the planning profession; in this situation the pattern of land use would have to be determined administratively, but 'planning' as a body of knowledge seems to offer no theoretically grounded technical criteria on the basis of which this might be done. (Reade, 1987 p.29).

As has been noted above, planners themselves have tended to be vague when identifying their cognitive competencies and skills. Moreover, at various times during the last fifty or so years, the planners' definitions of what constitutes the central expertise of the profession has changed as the purpose of planning as defined by the profession has changed. Thus, up until the 1950's, 'design' was claimed as a central skill - the capacity to create an environment which was functionally appropriate and aesthetically pleasing. As statutory planning expanded and the massive post-war redevelopment and slum clearance schemes proceeded, planning increasingly claimed a managerial competence - the ability to oversee a team of professionals in order to co-ordinate and implement policy.

In the 1960's much of the planning literature focused on systems theory, arguing that planning could harness the potential of computing in order to enable planners to model reality, and thus plan through technology (McLoughlin, 1969). The development of systems theory in planning seemed to offer the prospect of a planning based on technology, with planners as the holders of specific, technical skills in information technology applied to land use. However, it quickly became apparent that this approach was impossibly ambitious and impossibly naive in its attempt to technicise a complex social and political process (Healey, *et al.*, 1982). Latterly, planning has moved away from these grandiose claims to be a kind of environmental supra-profession and from its ambitious espousal of technology, towards a lower-key claim to an expertise in managing and manipulating the statutory planning system for both the public and private sectors. As Albrechts (1991) notes, planners now appear to be more concerned with how to plan, rather than with the outcomes of planning.

Despite the arguments that planning has no theoretical base, and that its claim to different kinds of expertise at different historical points is merely a reflection of its need to legitimise its professional status, the fact remains that planners' skills are in demand and can be sold on the market. In this sense they are an asset which can be utilised and exploited.

In what is possibly the only attempt to research the content of planning expertise, Healey and Underwood (1978) looked at local authority planners in three London Boroughs, and in this study they were concerned to understand the nature of planning ideas and knowledge as operated within an institutional context. Inevitably this involved the identification of the particular skills which planners employed in their day to day work, although this was not the primary aim of the research. Healey and Underwood concluded that in the cases studied, the kinds of knowledge being used by planners:

> were of standard procedures, of sources of literature, of information and advice notes, of ways of analysing particular issues (*e.g.* housing, employment and conservation) and of drawing out policy questions, and of ways of presenting information to different audiences (*e.g.* the council or the public). There was little evidence of the application of quantitative skills

> (other than tables), with the exception of a few people who were developing specialist knowledge in devising and running information systems. Skills in three dimensional design were only applied in specialist groups working on development problems. The impression was of individuals with varying collections of diffuse items of knowledge, sometimes related explicitly to some coherent framework of understanding of planning, but often not explicitly integrated and sometimes apparently inconsistent (Healey and Underwood, 1978 p.105-6).

They go on to argue that planners have little in the way of particular expertise:

> Any claim to 'expert' status, whether linked to professional institutions or not, would seem to require an association with knowledge and skills which have some specificity (not too general and vague, a clear object), some universality (applicable to a universe of problems), and some technical intricacy (more complex than a well-trained mind can handle). The knowledge and skills that were displayed by the planners studied here hardly satisfied such requirements (1978 p.121).

Turning to the question of how knowledge and skills were acquired by the planners studied, Healey and Underwood found that in most cases, planning education was seen as having little relevance, and that 'experience' was the main source of planning knowledge, in other words, knowledge that had been acquired in the course of working as a planner in one or more places. In two of the three case studies, planners saw 'professional channels' as important sources of knowledge and expertise, meaning their contacts with other professionals and reading the professional journals and magazines.

Healey and Underwood concluded that planning knowledge appeared to consist more of 'symbolic statements' rather than 'technical expertise' pointing out that its use in this symbolic way, frequently without the capacity to back up the symbol, had led to actual or anticipated 'crises of credibility'. This in turn led them to argue that "planners have acquired financial and occupational status on the basis of a variety of ideals, rather than recognised expertise" (p.122).

This review led Healey and Underwood to conclude that, in the case of local government planners implementing government policy, technical expertise is of rather less importance than a knowledge of various purposes of government in establishing such policy, knowledge of the means and effects of intervention by government and experience in defining and applying detailed policies and programmes. Thus, although the claim to a cognitive base is an important component of professionalisation, it is not a necessary element in actually doing what local government planners do, that is, implement an area of state policy.

The emphasis so far has been on the public sector where some 80% of planners are employed, but what of those who work in the development industry or as private consultants? As has been indicated above, it is likely that the existence of a clear client-expert relationship makes the position of this group easier in terms of identifying their role and purpose. Moreover, the definition of their expertise is also easier, in the sense that in many cases, they are often employed to secure planning permission. Whether this 'skill' is more legitimate than those identified in the public sector by Healey and Underwood is open to question, but it is clear that this is a marketable skill which until quite recently has been much in demand. However, not all planners in the private sector are employed in this way. A substantial proportion undertake projects and tasks not dissimilar from their colleagues in the public sector such as research work, plan preparation, feasibility studies and so on, although they do not, as yet undertake much development control work. Although no research has been undertaken on the skills employed by such planners it would seem reasonable to assume that these are somewhat similar to those employed by their public sector counterparts as discussed by Healey and Underwood.

Planning, professionalism and expertise

This review of the process and profession of planning has been undertaken in order to assess how one middle class occupational group has managed to secure its privileged position and status and to investigate the ways in which it has defined and utilised its asset of expertise in order to achieve this position. These questions will be reviewed further in the next two chapters, but before passing on to a consideration of the planners themselves, it is appropriate to briefly emphasise one or two points.

Although planning is widely regarded as a profession, and indeed has most of the formal trappings of professional status, in the conventional and popular usage of the term it really does not qualify. Its claim to cognitive competence does not stand up to close examination; it is an occupational group principally involved in administering state policy and thus cannot claim independent altruistic status; and it has a high degree of role confusion, particularly with regard to the identity of its clients. What is interesting about this is not the question of whether planning is or is not a profession according to some kind of trait approach definition, but how this particular middle class occupational grouping has managed to secure such privileges despite being unable to exhibit the characteristics normally associated with similar groups.

The answer to this must be that planning as a profession serves an important function in terms of managing a system of land use control which meets the needs of capital. The Institute has shown itself to be an effective body in regulating the 'expert' labour involved in this process, and it has also undertaken the intermediating functions appropriate to the corporatist role that it plays in relation to the state. In the context of these two circumstances, whether what planners do constitutes 'expertise' or not is largely an irrelevant question. The point is that planners have been legitimated to do what they do in return for agreeing to abide by certain ground rules. These rules are also likely to be enforced through the clan mode of regulation exercised principally by local authorities.

Throughout this chapter the discussion has focused upon the planning profession in a very general sense, and this means that, in effect, it has been a discussion of the attitudes and values of the 'professional community' of planning. In the next chapter, the emphasis will shift to a study of the general membership of this middle class occupational group, with a view to seeing how rank and file members of the profession view the processes that have been examined here, and to investigate the mechanisms and strategies that they utilise as individuals in order to secure their positions in society.

5 The planners

The previous chapter has examined the character of town planning as an activity of government, as a profession and as a reforming social movement. However in each of these cases the discussion has, inevitably, focused upon the attitudes, values and self-images of the profession as purveyed by the influential professional elite - in Laffin's terms the professional community - who are active in projecting the professions's interests to government, the public and influential institutions and organisations throughout society. It is difficult to judge exactly how many people comprise this professional community, but as Laffin points out, the numbers are likely to be small (Laffin, 1985). In the case of the Royal Town Planning Institute there are approximately forty or fifty members who are involved in the committee structure of the Institute, that is formulating Institute policy and representing the interests of the profession to various public and private sector bodies and to the general public. If influential members of the profession at the local level are included, it would not be unreasonable to argue that the professional community of planning currently comprises no more than perhaps one hundred people, mostly white men.

The focus of this chapter is not upon these high profile members of the town planning profession, although it is undoubtedly true that a few of the respondents to the questionnaires considered below are members of the professional community. Instead, this chapter examines the wider membership of the Institute by way of survey evidence, in order to shed light upon three areas of inquiry that have been considered in earlier chapters.

The first of these areas concerns class, and specifically the asset approach to class formation and analysis. Town planners are clearly members of a middle class occupation, however that might be defined, and they are equally clearly prime candidates for inclusion into any conception of the service class. Previous chapters have suggested how the notions of assets - economic, skill and organisation - might be understood and operationalised for public sector workers and professionals on the basis of existing research and empirical evidence. The problem is that much of this material tends to be rather general in character, and hence the survey material discussed within this chapter is an attempt to refine these perspectives and insights with reference to material derived from this one specific occupational group. Thus, town planners are examined here with a view to assessing the relative importance of the various assets to them as individual workers, employees and professionals.

The second area of inquiry relates to a number of issues which have emerged from the service class debate, notably the questions related to mobility and the relationship to locality; career patterns and the use of assets in promotion; and the potential splits within the service class between the public and private sectors, or the 'traditional' and 'new' service classes. An examination of this occupational group which spans both public and private sectors and which exhibits the utilisation of all three categories of asset, provides an opportunity to test some of the propositions which have been made within the service class debate.

Finally, these empirical investigations are directed towards understanding professionalism and professionalisation through an examination of the attitudes, values and self-images of the individual members of the occupational group, rather than through the pronouncements of the professional community.

The survey evidence considered in this chapter is derived from two main sources. Firstly there are the existing surveys of professional planners which were carried out in 1969, 1976 and 1988. Secondly there is the survey of planners in both the public and private sectors which was conducted in 1990 specifically for this study. Each of these sources will be examined in turn to see what insights may be revealed on the areas of inquiry noted above.

The existing surveys

The most recent survey of the general membership of the profession was commissioned by the RTPI and conducted at the end of 1988. It was a postal questionnaire, and effectively a census, of the Institute's Chartered membership. The results were published in the Institute's journal *The Planner* in 1990 (Nadin and Jones, 1990) providing a comprehensive profile of the membership in terms of income, demographic characteristics, employment status, qualifications and job responsibilities. The survey (henceforth referred to as the 'Profile' survey) did not investigate matters of attitudes, values or self-image.

A questionnaire was sent to every corporate member of the Institute, excluding retired members. Student members were not surveyed, nor were planners who were not members of the Institute, and of the 10,571 questionnaires sent out, 7,095 usable forms were returned, giving a response rate of 67%. This is a high response rate for a postal questionnaire, since expected responses are usually in the 20 - 50% range, but it reflects the socio-economic position of the respondents, in that response rates are usually higher amongst the middle class. It is also probably a reflection of the responsibility and commitment that members feel towards their professional institution. This high level of response means that the Profile Survey findings may be viewed as reliable.

The survey responses confirm that the typical Institute member is an:

> 'able-bodied', white European male, between 35 and 45 years of age, who works for a local authority in the south of England and earns between £12,000 and £20,000 (Nadin and Jones, 1990).

Women and members of black and ethnic minority groups are, not surprisingly, poorly represented. Only a handful of members based in Britain (less than half of one percent) described their ethnic origin as black, and although the Profile survey is silent on the employment status of these members, other studies have indicated that they will tend to be concentrated in the lower-paid and lower status positions (RTPI/CRE, 1983; Griffiths & Amooquaye, 1989).

Although there are more women in the profession - the survey indicated that nearly 15% of qualified planners are women - they again tend to be found principally in the lower status positions. Moreover, as Greed has pointed out (Greed, 1991), the actual number of qualified women planners in full-time employment is nearer 7%. This situation may be changing as women now make up 35% of the student membership of the Institute, but it is clear that planning, like the other land professions is still overwhelmingly dominated by men. For example, the Royal Institution of Chartered Surveyors has nearly 60,000 qualified members of whom 3% are women, while of the 28,000 members of the Royal Institute of British Architects, only 8.5% are women, of whom approximately 4% are in employment (figures from Greed, 1991).

The one land profession which does have a higher proportion of women members is the Institute of Housing with nearly 40% of its total membership being women. This occupational group has been in existence for longer than planning (at least since the mid-1850's and the pioneering housing management theories of Octavia Hill), but it has been markedly less successful in professionalisation than planning, and has yet to receive a Royal Charter. As several writers have pointed out, it is likely that this has been largely due to the fact that housing management has been represented as a female occupation, concerned with matters of domestic management which are somehow unworthy of professional designation (Brion & Tinker, 1980; Laffin, 1985; Roberts, 1991).

The Profile Survey emphasises that town planners are a highly credentialed occupational group. Over three-quarters (77%) of respondents hold an undergraduate degree, over half (54%) possess a Diploma in Town Planning while nearly one fifth (19%) have a Masters degree. Together, the 7,095 respondents share over 12,400 awards ranging from Higher Certificate to Doctor of Philosophy. Most planners (74%) do not hold another professional qualification, and of those that do, the most common is membership of the Royal Institution of British Architects (7%) and the Royal Institution of Chartered Surveyors (5%). These figures indicate that the process of professionalisation has secured independence for planners from the other, longer established land professions.

The survey confirmed that most planners still work in the public sector. About 65% work in local government, with a further 14% in education and 'other' public sector work - most probably central government, development corporations and nationalised industries. Around 20% of the membership work in the private sector, either in the development industry (for example private house building and property development companies or the retailing industry) or as private planning consultants in practices of varying size. The Profile Survey indicates that on the basis of an analysis of respondents' current and last posts, there has been a significant recent increase in private sector employment. In general, the public sector and the development industry have young age profiles with the largest proportion of respondents in the 35-39 age category. In contrast, the consultancy sector has a substantial proportion of older respondents, reflecting the tendency for senior local government staff to move into private consultancy later in their careers.

The mean salary for respondents in September 1988 was £18,583, although as the report on the survey points out the distribution of salaries is skewed with a small number of very high salaries lifting the mean.

> Salaries of full-time respondents range from well below £10,000 to over £100,000, indeed, there were a number of responses well in excess of that figure (Nadin & Jones, 1990).

As would be expected, planners in private consultancy tended to receive the highest salaries with a mean annual income of £22,727, compared with £18,227 for planners working for London Boroughs and £16,614 for employees of District Councils. It should be noted, however, that these lower public sector figures are in part a reflection of the younger age profile of this employment group.

Although the Profile Survey provides a reliable range of background information on certain characteristics of members of the planning profession, it is silent on questions relating to attitudes, values and self-image and it likewise does not provide information on their background or domestic circumstances. Some information on these questions is provided by two earlier surveys, the first carried out in 1969 (Marcus, 1971) and the second in 1976/77 (Knox and Cullen, 1981). These two, with the Profile Survey, appear to be the only surveys of planners to have been undertaken, with the exception of a small scale employment survey of members of the East of England Branch of the RTPI undertaken in 1984 (Cooper, 1984).

The survey undertaken by Marcus was based upon a random sample of 211 UK based members who had not retired. A total of 112 completed questionnaires were returned, representing a response rate of 52%. Although the Marcus survey, like the Profile Survey, did seek information on the make-up of the profession, in terms of qualifications, type of work undertaken, income, and membership of other professions, the main emphasis was upon collecting responses relating to views, values and attitudes. Although there did not appear to be any particular rationale behind the questions chosen, the responses provide a useful insight into attitudes within the profession twenty years ago.

In 1969, the social class background of planners was, in Marcus' words, 'undifferentiated middle class'. A large proportion of respondents' fathers, 46%, were in professional and executive occupations, while a further 29% were from middle and lower status white collar backgrounds. Less than twenty percent of respondents were from manual backgrounds. Interestingly, some two-thirds of the whole sample had fathers who had attended grammar or public schools. Despite these largely middle class origins, and the clear middle class status of the planning profession, the survey found that 31% of the sample were Labour Party supporters, 29% Conservative and 19% Liberal. This contrasted with a national Gallup poll held at the same time as the survey (April-May 1969) which revealed 31% for Conservative, 30% Labour and 13% Liberal, Bearing in mind the contemporary tendency for middle class voters to support the Conservative Party, the higher levels of support for non-Conservative parties amongst planners tends to confirm the existence of the reformist perspectives attributed to planners and planning the last chapter.

On average, the planners surveyed by Marcus had changed jobs six times. By the age of 31 there would have been two moves,with two more by the age of 41, one between the ages of 41 and 51 and one more after 51. Generally, the respondents had worked in five organisations by the end of their careers. This high rate of job mobility, compared with, for example, the mobility rates of graduates in industry at the same point in time (Craig, 1963), is complemented by a high rate of geographical mobility; only 27% of the sample had worked in only one region, whereas 13% had worked abroad at some time in their career. The survey also found that expectations of future moves were high in that, for example, only 34% expected to stay with their present employer until they retired.

Marcus found that the levels of satisfaction with work were high. In response to a request to state the satisfactions they found in their work, two main themes predominated. The first was the pride felt in the work itself, and the second was a desire to improve the quality of the physical environment around them. Over three-quarters of respondents mentioned one of these two satisfactions. Moreover, 84% of the sample stated that, given the opportunity to choose their career again, they would opt for planning. The only caveat expressed was that the majority of respondents ranked private practice higher than public sector work, perhaps, as Marcus suggested because 'the greater freedom enjoyed by private practice is appealing'.

The final survey is that carried out by Knox and Cullen (1981), and unlike the previous two, this research was based upon a theoretical perspective, in this case the urban managerialist thesis derived from a Weberian view of class and bureaucracy. Knox and Cullen examined the occupational group of planners in their role of urban managers, with a view to determining whether or not an 'institutional mind' could be identified. The importance of this to the managerialist thesis is that if such an 'institutional mind' exists within an occupational group, with homogeneous attitudes and patterns of behaviour, then it may be possible to evaluate the influence of particular managers on the 'urban system'. However, as numerous studies of 'gatekeepers' and urban managers demonstrated, it proved impossible to identify such a common value system or an institutional mind, and this was one of the main reasons why the managerialist thesis was subsequently abandoned (Norman, 1975; Williams, 1978). Knox and Cullen's survey did identify the existence of shared 'distinctive attitudinal orientations' amongst the planners surveyed, but their findings concerning the import of this for the managerialist thesis appear inconclusive. Nevertheless for the purposes of this study, the information on attitudes and self-image revealed by their study provides a useful source.

The survey involved interviewing sixty local authority planning officers of whom two-thirds were chief planning officers with the rest occupying various grades from deputy chief to assistant planning officer. Like Marcus, this survey emphasises the middle class nature and origins of planners, nearly half the sample having fathers in professional and managerial occupations. Knox and Cullen summarise the characteristics of the 'typical' planner on the basis of their interviews as follows:

> The average higher-echelon planner is very much a middle class animal. Aged between 31 and 35, he (for he is very much likely to be male), is likely to be married, to have children, and to live in a mortgaged house on a private residential estate. The typical planner will have progressed from grammar school (public school in a sizeable minority of cases) to university, generally in a Northern provincial city. Thereafter, he will have taken a job in a medium sized Borough. He will have stayed in the same local authority, or in a nearby authority, and is not likely to be a recruit from another profession. Like his parents, generally drawn from the professional and executive occupations, he admits to choosing the middle class as his objective social status. He will, in most instances, brave the elements to register his endorsement or dissatisfaction with the prevailing government, and is as likely to be a member of the local golf club as the local resident's association. (Knox and Cullen, 1981, pp.888-9).

In many senses this is an unsurprising picture, since it is largely a reflection of the style and characteristics of middle class life in late twentieth century Britain. There are, however, a number of points that require emphasis. Like the Marcus survey, this survey reveals the high level of credentialisation amongst the profession. The main difference is the reduced number of members holding two or more professional qualifications (mentioned above in the context of the Profile Survey), and the increasing proportion of university and polytechnic graduates who represent 80% of respondents. Sixty-five percent of these graduates held degrees in either geography or planning or some combination of the two, whilst social science subjects were poorly represented, sociology graduates for example constituting only 2% of the sample. This reinforces the point made by Ravetz who argues that it was geography, and not sociology as had originally been expected, that formed the academic base of town planning (Ravetz, 1986, p.56). Moreover it might be argued that the ethos and character of town planning as outlined in the previous chapter is reinforced by the assumptions and intellectual formulations of 'traditional' geography, whereas it is conceivable that graduates in other social science subjects might find this professional ethos uncongenial.

The Knox and Cullen survey is at odds with that of Marcus over the question of mobility. Whereas Marcus concluded that planners were highly mobile geographically, Knox and Cullen's results show that 43% of respondents work in the town of their birthplace, whilst a further 26% work in the same region as their birthplace. In terms of job mobility the figures are less clear. Although nearly 90% had been in their present position for less than two years, nearly 50% had been with their present local authority for 2-4 years, and 20% for more than ten years. Clearly, the statistics for job mobility must be treated with a degree of caution since they are a consequence of the demand for planners, which has fluctuated considerably during the last fifteen years, and of the associated consequences of various local government re-organisations which have tended to produce opportunities for promotion both within and between local authorities.

It is clear that the middle class are more enthusiastic joiners of local organisations than working class people (Janowitz and Kasarda, 1974; Willmott, 1986) and the Knox and Cullen survey demonstrates that planners are active locally. Nearly a quarter of respondents (23%) were members of a church group, while 15% were members of a parent-teacher association and a further 13% were in a residents' association. Overall 70% were members of some kind of local voluntary organisation.

Respondents were also more active in politics than the electorate as a whole with some 98% voting in elections compared with only 77% nationally. By the same token, the survey found that planners registered higher levels of interest in politics and were more likely to be members of political organisations (such as pressure groups) than the average, although they were less likely to members of political parties. This last is no doubt due to the reluctance of professionals to be seen to be politically committed, and perhaps to the existence of a local government culture which seeks to emphasise the technical and non-political role of officers. Like Marcus, Knox and Cullen found that the political allegiances of planners did not represent a startling departure from the electorate as whole.

Interestingly, when asked whether they held any strong political opinions, 45% replied in the affirmative, but only half of these were able to state what these strong opinions were, these ranging from 'right-wing' to 'socialist'. In the context of the work situation, 40% claimed to formulate their decision according to some specific perspective, which the majority defined in terms of 'humanist principles'. The second largest group described their approach in terms of a desire to bring about a redistribution of wealth in favour of the underprivileged groups. Overall, the survey reveals a starling level of confusion and political naivety amongst the respondents.

In response to the question 'to whom do you feel answerable for your decisions?', the majority nominated the electorate or, more often, its elected representatives rather than any professional or bureaucratic body. However, this deference to the power of the people, or the councillors needs to be put in context. A nominal responsibility to the electorate may be used as a rationalisation for actions and attitudes which might not find approval amongst the elected members. It is likely that professional planners have utilised exercises in public participation in this manner, perhaps to legitimise policies and courses of action which they felt were 'professionally' appropriate (Dennis, 1972; Boaden *et al.*, 1982).

The survey identified the existence of attitudes somewhat similar to these. One respondent states:

> "We are not lackeys of the politicians. In fact, part of our role is to check the tendency for personalities on council to get their own way."

Knox and Cullen found that some planners:

> tended to play down the abilities of council members, preferring to back their own judgement on most issues. In many cases, this attitude of benign cynicism was the product of years of experience in local authorities whose political status had frequently changed.

> This 'banana republic' environment seems to cultivate an avuncular sense of patronising tolerance, where council's demands are smilingly received, but quietly ignored. (Knox and Cullen, 1981, p.890).

The self-image of planners revealed by the survey reflects this attitude, Knox and Cullen argue that this self-image:

> sometimes reveals a smugness, its political altruism diluted with a worldly wise expediency. (p.889).

When asked to describe their professional aims, respondents tended to couch their answers in a kind of 'Platonic ideal' involving 'balance and harmony', answers being mainly divided between preserving the political and the environmental status quo. Thus, the planners interviewed tended to see themselves either as mediators - arbitrating between conflicting political forces - or as guardians of the environment. A third group emphasised the managerial role that planners play. Knox and Cullen also emphasise the planners' commitment to rationality:

> For planners, then, the city is paradoxical and puzzling; but the major response is one of a determination to rationalise this ambivalence and bring the world of appearances under the control of concrete, objective forces, (p.895).

Like the Profile survey and the Marcus survey, Knox and Cullen's work provides some useful insights into the attitudes and values of professional planners. However, in the context of the problems and issues outlined at the start of this chapter, all of these studies have limitations, not least of course, the fact that it is always necessary to exercise caution when statistics collected for one purpose are utilised for another. Although neither Marcus nor the Profile survey display any theoretical underpinnings, that of Knox and Cullen sought to pursue the then current urban managerialist debate. It is an open question as to how far the authors have tended to select data which confirms the existence of an 'institutional mind' or some kind of planning ethos, but it may be that the picture they construct of an altruistic, rational, patronising and somewhat naive profession may be an overstatement ten years on.

More generally, none of these studies provide information which permits an evaluation of the occupational grouping of planners in terms of the utilisation of assets, particularly skill assets or the development of career patterns. In addition, the questions related to uncovering information on political values is rather limited. In the light of these reservations concerning the existing studies, and the fact that they were becoming rather dated, it was decided to undertake a survey in order to provide empirical evidence which would address the problems outlined at the beginning of this chapter.

The 1990 survey

A postal questionnaire was sent out in July 1990 to 500 Chartered Town Planners, representing a sample of 5% of the total, non-retired, chartered membership of the Royal Town Planning Institute. It was initially intended that this sample should be drawn from the RTPI's membership list which at one stage was published annually. However, the Institute has recently decided to discontinue publishing this, and was not prepared to make a list available for research purposes. One problem with the RTPI membership list was that it did not identify members by place of work or employment status, and it was therefore impossible to sift out retired members, and more importantly for the purposes of this study, it would not have been possible to identify whether listed members were in the public or private sectors.

It was therefore decided to get the sample from two registers which list planners in the public and private sectors. The Directory of Official Architecture and Planning (29th edition, 1990) lists all public sector and quasi-public bodies in Great Britain which are involved in planning, development and architecture, for example, local authorities, local authority associations, development corporations and government departments. For each of these bodies, the senior professional staff are identified, and their responsibilities given. The level of detail tends to vary between authorities, and while some authorities only specify their most senior managers, others give details of their management hierarchy down to comparatively junior levels.

Given that approximately 80% of planners are employed in the public sector, it was felt that this Directory could provide an accessible and useful source of contacts for 80%, that is 400, of the postal questionnaires. Given the emphasis within the questionnaire upon career history and the utilisation of assets, it was necessary to ensure that respondents were at middle management level or above, since it is unlikely that younger, more junior officers could provide the information needed to assess the significance of assets in class analysis, or for that matter, to provide considered views on planning itself. It was therefore decided to concentrate upon officers at Principal Officer level and above, since this is the grade within local authorities which usually involve management responsibility and control of staff (organisation assets), higher salary levels (economic assets) and, presumably since virtually all respondents were professionally credentialised, skill assets. Given the different planning system in Scotland and Northern Ireland it was decided to restrict the survey to England and Wales, and given that the majority of planners are employed in local authorities, no public sector questionnaires were sent to employees of central government departments or statutory undertakers.

Names and work addresses were selected from the Directory at random, including a range of positions from middle to senior management, but ensuring that all were working within planning, and that as far as possible, all were chartered members of the Institute. In the event, virtually all respondents were professionally qualified, and most questionnaires were received by the person to whom they were addressed. However, the variety of procedures for dealing with incoming mail (there is little privacy in most local authorities) meant that in some cases the questionnaire was dealt with by another officer.

In a handful of cases this resulted in a reply but an uncompleted questionnaire. In a few cases it was returned with a note to the effect that officers were too busy. In others, the view was expressed that this was an impertinence that did not deserve a reply. However, in a great many cases, the Chief Planner took it upon him or herself to reply on behalf of the designated officer. Usually these replies were detailed and demonstrated the application of both time and care. In one or two cases only did the questionnaire get passed to the most junior member of the Department, presumably on the basis that this was a low priority.

Overall, the response to the questionnaires was extremely good. The response rate for the public sector was over 50%, and in the majority of cases, respondents completed it with considerable care. Considering that several of the questions could be viewed as intrusive - for example those asking about household income and share and property ownership - the responses were more than satisfactory. No doubt the complete anonymity of the questionnaire helped in this respect.

The remaining 20% of the questionnaires were destined for the private sector, and these were structured slightly differently from the public sector questionnaires in order to reflect the differences between the two sectors. The source for the private sector contact was the Royal Town Planning Institute's Directory of Planning Consultants (1990). Unfortunately, this does not include private sector planners working within the development industry (for example for property companies or volume house builders), but since this group represents only 4% of the Institute's total membership, and since the values, career patterns and utilisation of assets are likely to follow a pattern similar to consultants in private practice, it was felt that this was not a serious problem.

The Directory of Planning Consultants lists all consultancies registered with the Institute, and while some of these are comparatively large practices employing many chartered town planners as well as architects, surveyors, engineers and other professionals, many are small operations, often sole practitioners working alone. The directory lists these practices on a geographical basis, and the names and addresses were selected to reflect the regional distribution of practices and to ensure that a variety of sizes of firms were included.

Given that, compared with local authorities, most practices are small, the problems noted above of identified persons not receiving and responding to the questionnaire did not arise. The response rate was again good, being virtually the same as the public sector, the only difference being that some respondents were effectively retired or semi-retired, presumably using their practice as a means of keeping in touch and of supplementing income. Again, the respondents appear to have completed the questionnaire carefully, and there were no returned uncompleted forms. Presumably those who were too busy, or who found the questionnaire offensive, simply ignored it.

The questionnaire

The questionnaire was structured to elicit information on a number of subjects, principally the use and value of assets, career structures and geographical mobility, and attitudes towards, and views of the planning process and politics more generally. Although, for reasons of questionnaire design, the questions were not placed in the order outlined below, the questions were structured to address these issues in the following manner.

i Personal characteristics

Each respondent was asked to provide information on age, sex, father's occupation and self-assigned social class status. These general questions were necessary to provide background information to other data and also served as a check on the findings of previous surveys.

ii *Career details*

Information on present job was requested, linked to details of all planning jobs during the respondent's career. This question also asked whether it was necessary for the respondent to move in order to change job. Future expectations of job mobility were addressed as were attitudes to moving into the public or private sector of planning. These questions were designed to construct a picture of career patterns within the profession and to assess these in the light of the more general literature discussed in Chapter 2. In addition, this information is related to the questions on commitment to locality considered below.

iii *Skill assets and credentials*

Following on from the discussion in Chapters 3 and 4, these questions sought to determine firstly the actual skills utilised by planners, and to assist in judging whether it is credentials or skills *per se* that are important, and secondly to see if the skills demanded by the job change as respondents career developed. Thus, respondents were asked to provide details of qualifications and assessments of the skill requirements of their jobs, in addition to being asked to specify what they perceived as being the professional skills offered by town planners.

iv *Organisation assets*

As previous chapters have noted, the concept of organisation assets is rather vague. Nevertheless, in order to get some idea of the extent of these assets, respondents were asked to state how many staff they were responsible for. In addition, the question to public sector workers on attitude towards and potential job moves to the private sector, and the similar question (in reverse) to private consultants sought to assess how far organisation assets could be seen as transferable out of their organisational context. The questions on career noted above were also seen as providing information on this form of asset.

v *Economic assets*

Each respondent was asked to provide information on personal income, household income, the ownership of property in Britain and abroad, and share ownership.

vi Mobility and attachment to locality

The questions on career referred to above provide some information on this, but in addition, respondents were asked about their sense of attachment to the area where they live and for information on their membership of various local voluntary associations.

vii Views on the planning process

In order to investigate propositions relating to professionalism and professionalisation discussed in previous chapters, respondents were asked various questions concerning their views of the planning process, including their views on its purpose, the beneficiaries of that process, and to whom they feel responsible for the decisions that they take. These questions link closely to those of (viii) below.

viii Political attitudes

In addition to asking about respondents' voting intentions, the final section of the questionnaire asked for responses to a series of political propositions. These in part replicated the questions asked by Wright (1985) in order to assess class orientation, but they have had the more specific function of assessing the political attitudes held by planners in both the public and private sectors.

The remainder of this chapter outlines the survey results under these headings. In the following tables the 'raw', non-percentaged figures are given in parenthesis.

Personal characteristics of respondents

Of the 206 public sector respondents, 95% were male and 5% female, whilst in the private sector sample of 49 respondents, 84% were male and 16% female. These figures reinforce the general conclusion of the Profile survey considered above which was that women occupy only a tiny fraction of the senior planning posts in local government. In contrast, the proportion of women was higher in the private sector sample, and although the small size of the sample means that any findings have to be treated with a degree of caution, it may well be that private consultancy offers a degree of working flexibility which enables women to more easily combine work with domestic commitments. The private sector figure is very similar to the national figure produced by the Profile survey (see Table 5.1) and this may be because the private sector sample is less 'top-heavy' than the public sector sample, since it was not possible to accurately identify the sample's seniority from the source Directory.

Table 5.1
Town planners: gender

	Public sector		**Private sector**	
Male	95.0%	(196)	92.9%	(237)
Female	5.0%	(10)	7.1%	(18)
	100.0%	(206)	100.0%	(255)

The mean age for respondents was in the mid-40's, with the private sector respondents being marginally older on average at 45 years, compared with 43 years for the public sector. However, although the mean figures accurately reflect the public sector sample in that there were no very old respondents, the smaller private sector sample included one 83 year old who claimed to still be in practice! In the public sector sample (206) there were only three respondents aged 60 and over, and this probably reflects the tendency in recent years for local authorities to secure reductions in staff through early retirements. The slightly older average age of private sector respondents is in part a consequence of more senior public sector planners moving into private practice on retirement, either as employees of companies or as sole practitioners. There was no great difference between the two sectors in terms of experience in planning, with the public sector average being slightly lower at 19 years.

In response to the question 'Do you ever think of yourself as belonging to any particular social class?', nearly half of public sector and just over a third of private sector respondents replied in the negative. Of those who answered yes, most assigned themselves to the middle class, although nearly 5% of public sector respondents thought of themselves as working class (Table 5.2). These subjective class categorisations are not particularly surprising, but the reluctance of such a substantial proportion of respondents to assign themselves to any class does bear comment. When it is remembered that this is an educated and highly credentialised group, the majority of whom will have undertaken at least some elementary study of sociology as part of their professional studies, the refusal to recognise any class divisions is remarkable. It may well be that this is a reflection of the professional desire to be seen to be serving the interests of all sections of society noted in the last chapter, in which case any admission of class membership might imply partiality.

Table 5.2
Town planners: self-assigned social class

	Public sector		Private sector		All	
Working class	4.4%	(9)	0.0%	(0)	3.5%	(9)
Middle class	49.0%	(101)	59.2%	(29)	51.0%	(130)
No class	46.6%	(96)	36.7%	(18)	47.0%	(114)
Not stated/other	0.0%	(0)	4.1%	(2)	0.8%	(2)
	100.0%	(206)	100.0%	(49)	100.0%	(255)

Of course, this is not to imply duplicity or self-deception. It is quite clear from the responses to other parts of the questionnaire, which are discussed below, that many planners have a deep-seated belief in, and commitment to ideals of public service and altruism. Moreover, in the context of land-use planning these ideals often incorporate a vision of a world which is more equal and co-operative. In contrast, conceptions of class involve a recognition of inequality and usually of conflict to some degree, and this may be one reason why so many planners choose not to identify with the categorisations of social class.

Having said that, it may be significant that a smaller proportion of the private sector sample did not think of themselves as belonging to any particular social class, and that of those that did, virtually all identified themselves as middle class. This could be interpreted as a clearer statement of class awareness, or even consciousness, by this group, which in part may be a reflection of the more client-oriented rather than public service emphasis of the private sector of planning, which in turn may tend to de-emphasise the tensions described in the previous paragraph.

This discussion of subjective social class is conditioned by the fact that under most analyses, planners would be considered as members of a middle class or 'service class' occupation. The studies by Marcus and Knox and Cullen both concluded that the bulk of planners came from middle class backgrounds, but the results of this survey indicate that although a good proportion of the sample were born into middle class families, a significant percentage, around 40%, come from manual working class and routine white collar households (Table 5.3).

Table 5.3
Class origins of town planners

Father's occupation	Public sector		Private sector		All	
Manual working class	25.2%	(52)	20.4%	(10)	24.3%	(62)
Routine white collar	13.6%	(28)	24.5%	(12)	15.7%	(40)
Middle class	36.4%	(75)	51.0%	(25)	39.2%	(100)
Not clear	19.9%	(41)	0.0%	(0)	16.1%	(41)
No response	4.9%	(10)	4.1%	(2)	4.7%	(12)
	100.0%	(206)	100.0%	(49)	100.0%	(255)

Respondents were asked to state their father's occupation and these were then classified into the three broad categories of manual working class, routine white collar and middle class. Since the purpose here was to gain some general insight into social origins, rather than undertake a detailed study into mobility, it was felt that these broad (and admittedly a-theoretical) categories would serve. Only those occupations which could be unambiguously allocated to one of these three categories was recorded, and thus occupations such as 'civil servant' or 'local government officer' were excluded on the basis that they could fit into at least two categories. Similarly, problematic combinations such as 'artist and telephone operator', or 'journeyman felt hatter and youth worker' defied allocation. In contrast however, the majority of respondents provided occupational descriptions which were clear and unambiguous, such as carpenter, architect or miner (a sizeable number of respondents claimed to be the children of miners), and this may well be due to the fact that most planners have some experience of social survey work and thus of the placing of occupations into socio-economic categories.

On this basis 38% of public sector and nearly 45% of private sector respondents had fathers in either the manual working class or routine white collar categories, whilst 36% and 51% respectively came from middle class backgrounds. It has to be borne in mind that this sample of the profession is principally composed of more senior planners, who were educated and entered the profession during the 'long boom' of the 1960's and early 1970's. Thus they can be seen to be representative of a period in British post war history when the expansion of higher education and the public sector enabled many children of working class families to secure entry into higher status occupations.

Skill assets and credentials

As would be expected, virtually all respondents were either Members or Fellows of the Royal Town Planning Institute. The only exceptions to this were six public sector respondents, one of whom was a junior officer who had passed the Institute's examinations but had yet to apply for membership. Of the remaining five, one was a Chief Planning Officer of a District authority, one an Assistant Borough Planner and the remaining two were at Principal Officer level. Although these constitute only 3% of the public sector sample, their presence serves to remind that firstly, unlike medicine or law, there is no legal restriction on who can work as a town planner, and that secondly it seems possible that unqualified persons can competently undertake the professional responsibilities that go with a senior appointment in a local authority. That said, the survey evidence also clearly demonstrates that a professional credential is a necessary acquisition for career advancement, although as will be shown, not all planners are convinced that such qualification adequately prepares the holder for practice.

The Profile survey has demonstrated that planners are a highly credentialised occupational group and there was little point in asking questions which would simply duplicate the findings of this recent survey. Thus, apart from the questions on corporate membership considered above, the only request regarding credentials was that asking about membership of other professional institutions. The responses to this confirm that fewer planners are now qualified in planning and another built environment profession, and that overwhelmingly, a planning qualification is seen by employers as legitimate and valued credential on its own. Only a handful of the public sector sample are members of either the Royal Institution of Chartered Surveyors or the Royal Institute of British Architects, while approximately 7% of this sample belonged to some other professional institute, most commonly the Institute of Management. The private sector sample tended to have higher levels of dual professional membership, perhaps reflecting the need for both individuals and consultancy companies to secure maximum versatility in a commercial environment (Table 5.4).

Table 5.4
Membership of professional institutions

	Public sector		Private sector		All	
Royal Town Planning Institute	97.1%	(200)	100.0%	(49)	97.6%	(249
Royal Institution of British Architects	3.9%	(8)	14.3%	(7)	5.9	(15)
Royal Institution of Chartered Surveyors	6.8	(14)	12.2%	(6)	7.8%	(20)
Other (*e.g.* Inst. of Management, Inst. of Landscape Architects)	7.3%	(15)	16.3%	(8)	9.0%	(23)

(*NB:* Respondents may belong to more than one professional association.)

What does seem clear is that the credentials themselves are a very real and tangible asset which can be used to secure economic and organisation assets. Although, as will be discussed in the next chapter, 'there are plenty of PhDs driving taxis', and that possession of this asset does not necessarily mean that the asset will be exploited, in the case of planning it does seem to be the case that the actual qualification itself is of paramount importance in securing a high level of income and access to the advantages which are simply not available to non-credential holders. In this respect there seems to be little difference between the private and the public sectors.

Turning now to skills rather than credentials, respondents were asked: 'What in your view are the professional skills that Chartered Town Planners offer?' Responses were, inevitably, varied and thus difficult to categorise - a common problem of open-ended questions. However, a number of points emerged very strongly. Firstly, only a handful of respondents answered this question by making reference to specific skills or areas of knowledge, for example the operation of the Planning Acts and the associated semi-judicial processes; the preparation of land-use plans; the application of computer technology or the understanding of land markets and the development process. Although any of these might legitimately be seen as skills or knowledge relating to the process of planning, most respondents omitted to mention them.

In contrast, the majority of respondents chose to answer this question by referring to what might be termed 'general management' or 'interpersonal skills'. Thus phrases like 'ability to objectively assess requirements in the widest sense', or 'expert in multi-various activities' or 'the ability to take a broad scope and long term view of the competing needs of development and the environment' occur again and again. Co-ordination; synthesis; broad view; vision; negotiation; organisation - these are the terms that were incorporated in the overwhelming majority of responses. It was difficult to find a respondent who did not reply in these very general terms, and a great many answered the question by simply replying that the skills were 'too numerous to mention', or could simply described as 'an overview' or 'flexibility and adaptability'.

The flavour of the responses may be gained from a few examples:

> "An ability to take a broad view; analytical ability; contextual awareness." Chief Planner, 24 years experience.

> "General improvement to environment and living conditions through advice to committees and the public." Area Planning Officer, 36 years experience.

> "i) ability to balance conflicting views, ii) act in the public interest, iii) co-ordinate actions of others." County Planning Officer, 36 years experience.

> "Spatial awareness; the ability to marshall facts and present an argument; the ability to form judgments based on partial information and conflicting demands." Chief Planner, 16 years experience.

> "Awareness; assimilation of facts/details; analysis; problem solving." Chief Planning Officer, 23 years experience.

> "A balanced across-the-board knowledge of all the other professional inputs into the development process. To be able to see and appreciate the 'whole' picture." Chief County Planning Officer, 39 years experience.

A handful of respondents offered more precise statements of the planner's skills, but even here the specific is often overwhelmed by the more general:

> "Some planners bring individual and specific skills to the profession, but the main skill of a planner is to be able to synthesise and assess complex problems and produce a logical, socially and politically acceptable solution!" Deputy Planning Officer, 21 years experience.

> "Assembly of relevant data, analysis and critical evaluation of competing demands and subjective value judgments (sic) on all environmental issues. A thorough knowledge of planning law and national planning policies." Chief Planning Officer, 30 years experience.

These quotations are totally representative of the responses to this question, and apart from a few, like the person who replied 'a sense of humour and a thick skin!', virtually all defined the planner's professional skills in these general, over-arching, managerial terms.

A number of points need to be made about these responses. Planners have been widely criticised for their alleged tendency to assume the mantle of a kind of super-profession, seeking to manage and co-ordinate the actions and activities of others without any legitimate justification for this (Reade, 1987). In addition, it has often been argued that many planners have tended to adopt an attitude of almost god-like superiority which convinces them that only they have the overall interests of the community, the public or the environment in view. It was this attitude that Davies addressed in this study of planners as 'evangelistic bureaucrats' (Davies, 1972).

It is possible to regard these kinds of criticism of planners as overstated and possibly outdated, and to question their validity in that there has been virtually no empirical research designed to test these assertions, which have largely been based on case studies and assessments of the pronouncement of the professional community of planning. However, a reading of the sample's responses to this question leaves little doubt that these kinds of attitudes and views still have wide currency amongst professional planners. A related criticism of planning, which was discussed in the last chapter, has been its inability to develop a coherent body of theory to underpin its practice. Unfortunately, there is nothing in the responses to this question to suggest that planners are aware of, or feel the need for any theory in their professional lives.

The responses to this question also clearly confirm the findings of Healey and Underwood (1978) which were discussed in the last chapter. In their study of three local authority planning departments, Healey and

Underwood found that the planners did not display or utilise technical expertise in the course of their work, and that the skills they used did not qualify for the categorisation of 'expertise'. Rather, concluded Healey and Underwood, in the case of the planners employed in the public sector, technical expertise is of rather less importance than a knowledge related to operating and implementing state policy.

The responses of the sample to this question clearly reinforces this conclusion, and it is interesting to note that there is no discernible difference between the responses from the public and private sector samples. It might be expected that clients are prepared to engage planning consultants because of their particular skills, for example in securing planning consent for particular development proposals, and in this respect at least, it might be reasonable to argue that private sector planners do possess particular tangible and marketable skills. However, this did not appear in the responses to the question, which may be a result of the power of the professional ideology of planning and the notions of altruistic service which have been discussed earlier, and the influence of these over planners in both employment sectors. In other words, private sector planners might feel that their status as independent, professional experts might be threatened if they were to perceive themselves, or allow others to see them as, simply providing a service to clients (usually the development industry and property owners), rather than operating in the interests of the public, the community or the environment.

It might be argued that the responses described above would be expected from a sample of senior professionals, the majority of whom are in managerial positions. Thus, they would be expected to be spending most if not all of their time on managerial matters rather than professional matters, and indeed, in response to the question 'have the skill requirements of your job changed as you have achieved more senior positions in planning?', most respondents replied in the affirmative, citing the increasing importance of management skills as the main change. Nevertheless, this does not detract from the fact that the questionnaires asked what are 'the professional skills that town planners offer?'. It would not be difficult to imagine the kinds of response to a similar question put to senior civil engineers, lawyers or accountants.

The final question concerning credentials and skills requested respondents to think back to their planning studies, asking if they felt that they constituted adequate preparation for practice. There was a considerable difference between the two sectors here, in that whereas nearly 60% of private sector respondents answered 'yes' to this, only 37% of public sector planners thought that their studies had prepared them adequately. Those that had answered 'no' to this question were invited to say why, and although it would not be possible to draw many firm conclusions from these responses - too many different forms of training and education are involved including full-time undergraduate, part-time postgraduate and correspondence courses, taken over a thirty year period - a number of points clearly emerged.

A high proportion of respondents to this question stated that in their view their studies had been too theoretical or too academic. In the same vein, many thought that there had been insufficient coverage of 'practical' issues relating to the day-to-day work of the planner. Both of these points emerged sufficiently regularly in these responses to raise an important point about the relationship between planning education and planning practice.

If planning education were to become more practically oriented, and to concentrate upon simply providing the knowledge necessary for practice - for example, the operation of the planning legislation, statutory procedures, design and development control practice - it may well be that academic institutions will become reluctant to award degrees at undergraduate and postgraduate level for this, preferring instead to opt for lower status 'technical' qualifications to reflect a 'practical' rather than 'theoretical' emphasis. However, as has been pointed out in earlier chapters, the process of professionalisation invariably involves legitimation through the acquisition of higher status credentials, usually at undergraduate and postgraduate level, which in the case of planning has meant that curricula have tended to become more 'academic' and theoretical' in character.

Thus, there is a tension here. If this sample is representative, it seems probable that many practising planners feel that their planning education was too theory-laden and academic, and lacking in practical detail. Moreover as Healey and Underwood (1978) found, most of the planners in their case studies obtained their planning knowledge from 'experience' or on-the-job learning, rejecting planning education as having little relevance. However, as Larson, Johnson and others have pointed out (Johnson, 1972; Larson, 1977), professionalisation inevitably involves legitimation through credentials which declare that the occupational group has a distinctive cognitive competence. In addition, professional status (and the higher rewards that accompany this) are in part legitimised by the length and level of the professional training received. (Larson makes the point that this means that professionalism is inevitably characterised by overtraining). Thus, to make planning education more 'practical' would also be to threaten the professional status of the occupation.

Economic assets

The process of professionalisation may in part be seen as a mechanism for achieving the maximum price for the sale of expert labour, and in this sense it is clear that town planners have achieved this objective. In both the public and private sector samples, the majority of respondents were earning between £20,000 and £30,000 per annum from their planning jobs (Table 5.5). Of course, it has to be recognised that these figures represent the kind of salaries which more experienced and senior planners receive, but given the normal career patterns of planners, these figures represent the salaries which most planners are likely to secure during the course of their working lives. Some respondents however, were in receipt of considerably higher salaries, with approximately 16% of private sector and 6% of public sector salaries in the £35,000 and over category.

Thus, in terms of the sale of their expert labour, the sample appear to be well remunerated, even though many of them - particularly those in the public sector - may not agree. However, when the income of the sample is considered in term of household income, rather than just the salary received for the planning job, levels rise dramatically.

Respondents were asked to state whether another member of the household was employed, and whether this was full or part time. They were then asked for their total household income inclusive of all salaries, returns on investment and so on. They were also asked whether they were an owner occupier and whether they owned any shares, or other land or property either in the UK or abroad. Together these pieces of information help to construct a picture of the overall income of respondent's households.

As might be expected, virtually all the sample were owner occupiers, although how many were outright owners, and what outstanding mortgage commitments exist was not investigated. Moreover, it was not possible to collect information of house value in order to assess the extent of capital ownership in the dwelling. Nevertheless, it is reasonable to assume that the majority of the sample are benefiting from the normal advantages which accrue to owner-occupiers in Britain, and that they will therefore usually possess a considerable economic asset which may be traded to release capital for other purposes.

Table 5.5
Salaries and household income

Salary

	Public		Private		All	
Under £10,000	0.0%	(0)	4.1%	(2)	0.8%	(2)
£10-15,000	0.5%	(1)	12.2%	(6)	2.7%	(7)
£15-20,000	18.0%	(37)	10.2%	(5)	16.5%	(42)
£20-25,000	37.8%	(78)	26.6%	(13)	35.7%	(91)
£25-30,000	23.3%	(48)	20.4%	(10)	22.7%	(58)
£30-35,000	13.6%	(28)	6.1%	(3)	12.2%	(31)
£35,000 +	5.8%	(12)	16.3%	(8)	7.8%	(20)
No response	1.0%	(2)	4.1%	(2)	1.6%	(4)
	100.0%	(206)	100.0%	(49)	100.0%	(255)

Household income

	Public		Private		All	
Under £10,000	0.0%	(0)	0.0%	(0)	0.0%	(0)
£10-15,000	0.0%	(0)	0.0%	(0)	0.0%	(0)
£15-20,000	7.3%	(15)	4.1%	(2)	6.7%	(17)
£20-25,000	18.9%	(39)	18.4%	(9)	18.8%	(48)
£25-30,000	22.4%	(46)	14.3%	(7)	20.8%	(53)
£30-35,000	18.9%	(39)	12.2%	(6)	17.6%	(45)
£35,000 +	20.6%	(63)	44.9%	(22)	33.4%	(85)
No response	1.9%	(4)	6.1%	(3)	2.7%	(7)
	100.0%	(206)	100.0%	(49)	100.0%	(255)

Around 40% of both samples owned shares (44.8% private sector; 37.8% public sector) although it is not known how extensive this ownership is. A few respondents were at pains to indicate that their share ownership was involuntary and a consequence of building society share flotations. A quarter of private sector respondents claimed to own land or property in addition to their house while only 11.6% of the public sector sample were in this position. In the case of both of these assets, shares and property, income may result, depending upon the circumstances, and this may be quite substantial. The point about these figures however, is that they simply indicate the ways in which this comparatively privileged occupational group may hold economic assets, whether they have been purchased through income or as a consequence of inheritance.

The majority of respondents had another member of their household in paid employment which of course, has the effect of considerably boosting the total household income. Table 5.5 shows that in both the public and private sector, the majority of respondents' household income was in excess of £30,000 per annum, 57% of households in the private sector and nearly 50% in the public sector. In both sectors, approximately 70% of respondents had another member of their household in paid employment, the main difference being that the proportions in full time and part time employment were reversed for each sector (Table 5.6).

Table 5.6
Percentage of respondents with another member of the household in paid employment

	Public sector		Private sector		All	
In full-time employment	29.1%	(60)	46.9%	(23)	32.6%	(83)
In part-time employment	40.8%	(84)	30.6%	(15)	38.8%	(99)
One-income H/H	30.1%	(62)	22.5%	(11)	28.6%	(73)
	100.0%	(206)	100.0%	(255)	100.0%	(255)

The general picture is thus of two-income households where a combination of earned and unearned income provides a high overall annual total, and where the ownership of capital assets - principally owner-occupied housing, but also shares and property - is high. In this sense the sample may be regarded as a financially secure and privileged occupational group, and it may well be that the possession of these economic assets provides a degree of independence, particularly to those older (and presumably more financially secure) members of the profession. For those in the public sector, this financial independence can cushion against early retirement and redundancy. Moreover, public sector planners subjected to these processes may well have the option of moving into consultancy, often on a sole practitioner and part time basis. Indeed, many respondents mentioned this as a likely course of action. Private sector planners may be more vulnerable to the vagaries of the market, but the possession of these economic assets will certainly soften the blow of redundancy or loss of business.

Organisation assets

Organisation assets are perhaps most readily defined as mechanisms which may be manipulated, explicitly or implicitly, in order to ensure that the organisations' resources or actions benefit particular broad social groups in society, usually the middle or service class, and it was this perspective on organisation assets which was examined in Chapter 3. This process occurs as part of the normal procedures and activities of an organisation, and it is particularly likely to happen in the case of public sector organisations, most obviously, local authorities.

However, organisation assets may also be utilised or manipulated by asset holders to secure benefits for particular specified individuals or groups, but this would normally constitute some kind of illegal action or corruption and is thus outside of the purview of this investigation. The exception to this would be the use of the organisation's resources to benefit the individual resource controller in a legal and acceptable manner - examples might be health service workers receiving favourable medical care for themselves or their families, or town planners' familiarity with proposed planning schemes enabling them to select preferred residential locations. It is this latter perception of organisation assets that Wright seems to be referring to in his formulation discussed in Chapter 2 (Wright, 1985), but these are, by their very nature, difficult to quantify and assess.

These perspectives on organisation assets emphasise that the controller or holder of the assets can only achieve benefits from the assets if she or he is employed by the organisation. To leave is to relinquish control and to lose benefit. However, it is clear that some employees who control organisation assets - for example managers of public sector policy programmes, computer services managers or oil company executives - gain organisational knowledge (as opposed to expert or technical knowledge) whilst they are in their positions of authority. This knowledge may well be very specific and will relate primarily to a detailed understanding of how organisations operate, both formally and informally. If an employee leaves an organisation and then seeks new employment where this particular experience and knowledge is employed, what is happening is that organisation assets are being traded for economic assets, perhaps in the form of skill assets. Nevertheless, regardless of the terms that are selected to describe the process, it seems likely that certain occupations within, usually large, organisations may be accruing a valuable asset which can be sold to competitors within the industry, or more likely to other providers or users within the same general business.

Thus, examples of this process might be consultants in the petro-chemical industry advising suppliers of refinery plant and equipment who are seeking to sell their product to the large multi-national oil companies. Knowledge relating to decision processes, purchasing procedures, technical specifications, compatibility with existing systems and so on, would be gained by senior employees in certain sections of the industry as part of controlling a large organisation. For obvious reasons this insider knowledge may become very valuable and may be sold via consultancy.

A somewhat similar example is the practice of large companies recruiting newly retired senior civil servants and cabinet minsters. It may be that they are being employed because of their particular skills, but is seems likely that they are also in possession of another major asset, that of insider knowledge of the functioning of a particular organisation.

In the case of town planning, there has been a regular movement of senior local government personnel into the private sector of planning, either on early retirement or in mid-career. This process seemed to reach a peak during the development boom of the last half of the 1980's when volume house builders and development companies in particular were eager to recruit experienced local authority planners. In part this was a reflection of a booming industry and a consequent shortage of skilled labour. However, it also seems likely that a good proportion of the planners who made this move were recruited because they could offer knowledge of the operation of local authority planning processes on the basis of experience. In other words they knew how the system worked in some detail - formally and informally - and they may even have been able to offer some insider information on future prospects for development or otherwise, and a range of personal contacts both professional and political. The asset they have to offer in these cases is based upon their organisational position, and it is this which is likely to be the principal asset sold on the market, rather than their skill, since, as has been already emphasised, the skills that planners have, at the senior level in particular, are likely to be non-specific and managerial in character. It would therefore seem to be appropriate to designate these assets as being principally organisational in character.

However, an asset, whether it be economic, skill or organisation, only has any significance if it is utilised or exploited in some way. Given the discussion of organisation assets above, how likely is it that planners will exploit these assets? Table 5.7 shows the public sector experience of the private sector sample by recording their most senior local government post, derived from the question which asked for their career history. Although there is some difficulty in judging how senior a post a title such as 'principal officer' or 'senior officer' represents, since designations vary between local authorities, the responses do provide a number of insights.

Table 5.7
Public sector planning experience of private sector respondents (percentage of respondents by most senior local government post held).

Planning Assistant	22.4%	(11)
Senior Planner	18.4%	(9)
Principal Planner	26.5%	(13)
Assistant Chief/Director/Chief Planning Officer/	16.4%	(8)
Director of Planning	2.0%	(1)
No public sector experience	6.1%	(3)
No response/unclear	8.2%	(4)
	100.0%	(49)

Firstly, as would be expected, most of the sample has some experience of working in the public sector, with only two respondents never having worked for local authorities, and one having done so but not in the UK. The largest group of respondents had experience of local authority planning at Principal Officer level and above. This means that they were most likely to have been in a supervisory or managerial position, responsible for the work of other professional planners, with regular contact with elected members and other senior council officers. Indeed, some 18% of the sample had been Chief Planning Officers or Deputies in their last local authority post.

However, this must be balanced by the fact that nearly one quarter of the sample (22%) only had experience of public sector work at the most junior level, that is Planning Assistant, whilst a further 18% left local government when they were Senior Officers, the grade immediately above planning assistant. Although such people would be taking some experience and skills to the private sector, it is difficult to imagine that they would have had the level of experience necessary to permit them to be transferring out organisation assets in the manner described above. Thus, on the basis of this admittedly small sample of private sector planners, it is likely that just over 40% could be viewed as having transferred organisation assets out into the private sector.

All of the public sector sample were asked whether or not they would be prepared to consider taking a job in the private sector of planning, and to indicate the reason why. The responses to this were fairly equally divided in that just over half the respondents stated that they would consider a private sector job while 43% said they would not, with 6% not responding or uncertain (Table 5.8). The most common reasons for being prepared to accept a private sector post were 'career reasons', for example that the respondent would like a new challenge, or a change, or would simply wish to be to open all career options.

Table 5.8
Future mobility to the private sector by public sector planners

		Yes		No		Don't know	
i)	Would you consider a job in the private sector of planning?	50.9%	(105)	43.3%	(89)	5.8%	(12)
ii)	If yes, why?						
	a) more money or perks	15.2%	(16)				
	b) less political interference	7.6%	(8)				
	c) dissatisfaction with present position	5.7%	(6)				
	d) retiring shortly	17.2	(18)				
	e) career reasons (*e.g.* new challenge, need for change	37.1%	(39)				
	f) unclear/not stated	17.2%	(18)				
		100.0%	(105)				

iii)	If no, why?		
	a) happy in present post	6.7%	(6)
	b) commitment to public service	53.9%	(48)
	c) material considerations (*e.g.* pensions)	27.0%	(24)
	d) unclear/not stated	12.4%	(11)
		100.0%	(89)

The second most common reason was that the respondent was about to retire, or was in the latter stages of a career, and would welcome the opportunity to shift into consultancy, most probably sole practice. A number of replies referred to the desirability of moving into a more independent environment, free of 'political interference', whilst an equal number articulated their disenchantment or dissatisfaction with local government or their present post. A similar number stated that they were attracted to the private sector because of the higher salaries and more generous fringe benefits and 'perks'. It is worth mentioning that a number of respondents appeared to be offering a reluctant 'yes' to this question, in that they perceived planning to be experiencing what they regarded to be an inevitable shift to the private sector, and in these circumstances, perhaps where many local authority planning functions would be privatised, some respondents would see applying for private sector jobs as inevitable. Additionally, several respondents mentioned that they felt they possessed experience and knowledge which would be of value to the private sector, and one volunteered the information that he had been approached by private sector firms with job offers on two occasions, but for personal reasons he had declined. He noted with some bitterness that this 'headhunting' had not had the effect of increasing his local government salary!

The respondents who did not wish to move to the private sector offered a variety of reasons in explanation, the most common of which was a stated commitment to local government, 'public service' or 'serving the community'. Many of these responses articulated the view that the true role of planning was in the public sector, and that they had no wish to become the agents of developers, or placed in a position where the interests of the client would force a compromise of professional judgement (Table 5.8). The other major reason for not wishing to enter the private sector can be summarised as 'material considerations'. Many respondents wished to protect pension rights, whilst others mentioned the vulnerability of the private sector and what one respondent referred to as the 'uncongenial lifestyle' of private sector planners.

Most planners in the private sector sample (61%) did not wish to return to the public sector, and many expressed their reasons for this quite forcefully. 'I've done my stint with local authorities - life is more stimulating in the private sector', wrote one respondent. Another was more blunt; 'Poor working conditions, general flabbiness of local government - UGH!'. These responses were perhaps to be expected, but they were balanced by the nearly one third of the private sector sample who did consider a public sector job a possibility. Many of these respondents were quite clear that a return to the public sector would only be possible for them under the right circumstances, for example 'providing it had a reasonable chance of making an improvement to the environment and a decent remuneration', as one respondent put it. In general though, the majority of these responses indicated a view that, although respondents would be prepared to consider a public sector post, it would have to quite exceptional to improve upon the working conditions and remuneration of the private sector.

It is also worth noting that, although many private sector respondents preferred their sector because of its higher salaries and superior fringe benefits, the overwhelming majority of the respondents emphasised the stimulation, independence and freedom of the private sector, compared with what they viewed as the bureaucratic, mechanistic and politically restrictive public sector working environment. A typical response to the question asking why the respondent did not wish to return to the public sector was because there was;

> "no sense of achievement - in the private sector you are accountable for all your actions. You see a job through from beginning to end. Also you can act on your own initiative and not keep consulting other senior planners or elected members as to the right decision," (planner with 12 years public sector experience).

Another commented;

> "I consider that public sector planning is at its lowest ebb since the early 1950's (possibly since the operation of the 1947 Act). The main impetus is now in the private sector and is likely to remain there for some time," (ex-Assistant Director with 25 years public sector experience).

Turning now to present posts, virtually all public sector respondents were responsible for the work of other staff, and in some cases for the work of whole Departments or Directorates with up to 100 staff. This, of course, was to be expected, given the selection of the sample, but it does emphasise the extent of organisation assets in terms of formal power and influence over the work of other employees. Surprisingly, perhaps, many of the private sector respondents also worked in larger organisations where they had responsibility for the work of other professional and administrative staff. Most however, some 70%, were employed in companies or partnerships with less than five professional planners.

Career, mobility and attachment to locality

As would be expected from a sample of this nature, all respondents had experienced promotion during their careers, and many were at the peak of their profession as Chief Planners, Directors of Development or Senior Partners in private practice. Virtually all had moved house as a consequence of a career move, and in most cases this had happened two or three times. A range of questions were posed which were designed to ascertain how far respondents felt attached to the areas where they lived, and to see if this would prevent them from moving in order to secure a new job. It was expected that this information would provide insights into constraints on job mobility and the social networks of the middle class professionals in the areas where they live.

The survey results confirm Knox and Cullen's findings that planners tend to be active in their localities, and that they are joiners of local organisations and associations. The majority of respondents in both sectors were members of local organisations, such as a church group, residents association, Round Table, sports club or parent-teacher association, and a significant proportion of respondents were members of two or more groups (Table 5.9).

Table 5.9
Respondents' membership of local organisations

	Private sector		Public sector		All	
Member of 1 organisn.	37.9%	(78)	44.9%	(22)	39.2%	(100)
Member of 2 organisns.	18.0%	(37)	18.4%	(9)	18.0%	(46)
Member of 3 organisns.	7.8%	(16)	16.3%	(4)	9.4%	(24)
Member of 4 organisns.	2.9%	(6)	0.0%	(0)	2.4%	(6)
Member of 5+ organisns.	1.9%	(4)	0.0%	(0)	1.6%	(4)
None/no response	31.5%	(65)	20.4%	(10)	29.4%	(75)
	100.0%	(206)	100.0%	(49)	100.0%	(255)

Respondents were asked if they felt a strong sense of attachment to the area where they lived, to which question some three-quarters of the sample replied 'yes' (Table 5.10). These respondents were then asked if this attachment would prevent them from moving to a job in another area, and in both sectors only about 20% agreed that it would. However, a further 25-30% thought that this would 'probably' be a barrier to moving, resulting in a sizeable proportion of respondents who felt sufficiently attached to their neighbourhood to state that this *might* affect their career ambitions. There did not seem to be any correlation between those who had children of school age living with them and those who expressed a wish to remain in their existing neighbourhood. In general though, the respondents who were prepared to consider a job move which would take them away from their present locality were in the majority.

Table 5.10
Attachment of respondents to locality

Do you feel a strong sense of attachment to the area where you are currently living?

	Public sector		Private sector		All	
Yes	78.6%	(162)	75.6%	(37)	78.0%	(199)
No	11.2%	(23)	12.2%	(6)	11.4%	(29)
Indifferent	10.2%	(21)	12.2%	(6)	10.6%	(27)
	100.0%	(206)	100.0%	(49)	100.0%	(255)

If yes, would this prevent you moving to a job in another area?

	Public sector		Private sector		All	
Yes	20.4%	(33)	18.9%	(7)	20.1%	(40)
No	48.8%	(79)	56.8%	(21)	50.3%	(100)
Probably	30.8%	(50)	24.3%	(9)	29.6%	(59)
	100.0%	(162)	100.0%	(37)	100.0%	(199)

Most of the younger and middle-aged respondents expected to have a new planning job within the next five years, confirming Marcus' findings that planners tend to have high expectations of job mobility. Of those who expected to move in this period, the majority were prepared to move house in order to secure a job. Those who were not prepared to accept a job which would necessitate moving house were invited to give their reasons, and although there were not a large number of replies to this, those that there were tended to emphasise family commitments as the reason for remaining in an area. Several responses were phrased in such a way as to suggest that the respondent would be prepared to move, but that his or her family would not be willing to do so, or that obligations such as childrens' schooling would prevent a move. Only a small proportion expressed views similar to the respondent who replied; 'my home life is more important than my career, in terms of a move'.

Although these figures must be treated with some caution, it is probably reasonable to state that they emphasise the commitment of the middle class to the localities where they live, and that this is likely to be manifested in terms of joining various local groups and associations, as well as in other more informal ways. This largely restates established sociological wisdom, but what is perhaps more important for the purposes of this study is that this commitment to locality does not appear to be so over-riding that it would be likely to prevent a career move to another area. Moreover, in the case of planners, there appears to be little difference in these terms between public and private sector employees, or between those members of the service class depending primarily upon organisation assets and those depending primarily upon skill assets (Savage, *et al.*, 1988).

Views on the planning process

Perhaps the first point to note is that most respondents felt optimistic about the future of the planning profession. Just over 80% of the private sector and nearly three-quarters of the public sector samples replied positively to a question asking about this, and when invited to explain why, most stated either that society is becoming more environmentally aware, and that planning would therefore become progressively more important, or that the last decade of privatisation and deregulation had failed to have any substantial impact upon planning and had thus demonstrated the necessity for some kind of land use regulatory system despite the political complexion of the government in power. Thus most saw this question in political terms, with a few specifically replying that; 'Thatcher cannot last forever' or 'I'm optimistic now that Ridley's gone'.

The minority who were not optimistic felt that the last ten years in particular had seen an erosion of local authority planner's powers and had been a period when planning generally had taken a back seat relative to the interests of landowners and the development industry. A few public sector planners had their optimism blunted by the undoubtedly difficult circumstances within which most local government employees at present work.

The questionnaire asked; 'in your work to whom do you feel ultimately responsible for your decisions?', (Table 5.11). Public sector respondents were prompted with the categories of the elected members, the general public or 'other, please specify'. In the case of the private sector sample, 'the elected members' was replaced by 'the client'. Nearly 60% of the public sector sample stated that they felt ultimately responsible to the elected members; 'after all', reasoned one; 'they pay my salary'. Just over 50% of the same sample (many respondents gave more than one category in answer to this question) specified 'the general public', again raising the point discussed earlier that the altruistic ethos of the profession as serving the 'public interest' permit planners to take the view that the wishes of their democratically elected councillors may be set in the context of what the planner defines as the 'public interest' or the 'general good'.

Table 5.11
Professional responsibility

In your work, to whom do you feel ultimately responsible for your decisions?

	Public sector		Private sector	
The elected members	57.7%	(119)	N/A	
The client	N/A		67.3%	(33)
The general public	51.9%	(107)	24.4%	(12)
The profession/self	6.3%	(13)	14.2%	(7)
Other	3.8%	(8)	4.0%	(2)

NB: More than 1 response per questionnaire

This view was less prevalent in the private sector sample where less than one quarter of respondents mentioned the general public. In contrast, and as would perhaps be expected, nearly 70% expressed a clear loyalty to the client - the individual or organisation who pays the bills. However, a sizeable minority stated that they were ultimately responsible to themselves or their profession, which to an extent is a similar response to nominating 'the general public'. In contrast only 6% of the public sector sample gave their profession or 'myself' in answer to this question. Most respondents from both sectors replied by nominating one of the above categories, although there were a few exceptions. One or two public sector planners nominated their Chief Planner or Chief Executive, whilst one respondent, perhaps taking the question too literally, replied; 'Our Lord'.

All respondents were then asked to state whether or not they thought the planning process benefits any specific groups in society. A majority in both sectors (64% public sector and 53% private sector) though that it did, and these respondents were invited, in an open ended question, to specify who these groups might be. Table 5.12 outlines the responses to this and shows that the majority of replies in both sectors identified developers and land and property owners as the major beneficiaries of planning. The second largest group to be identified were the 'well-educated' or the 'articulate middle class'. These categories were identified without prompting by a significant proportion of the samples. In addition, many identified 'pressure groups and objectors', a category which is likely to largely comprise of middle class people.

Table 5.12
Beneficiaries of the planning process

i) Does planning benefit any specific groups in society?

	Public sector		Private sector		All	
Yes	64.1%	(132)	53.2%	(26)	62.0%	(158)
No	28.6%	(59)	34.6%	(17)	29.8%	(76)
No response	7.3%	(15)	12.2%	(6)	8.2%	(21)
	100.0%	(206)	100.0%	(49)	100.0%	(255)

ii) If yes, who benefits?*	Public sector		Private sector	
1) Property owners/developers	48.8%	(64)	50.0%	(19)
2) The articulate middle class	36.3%	(48)	15.7%	(6)
3) Pressure groups/objectors	9.8%	(13)	10.5%	(4)
4) Local residents	6.8%	(9)	7.9%	(3)
5) Less powerful/disadvantaged	4.5%	(6)	2.6%	(1)
6) The general public	9.8%	(13)	13.1%	(5)
7) Others	7.6%	(10)	0.0%	(0)

*NB: More than 1 response per questionnaire

These responses are interesting not for their revelations - they are merely confirming what social scientists have been stating for many years - but for the fact that the 'rank and file' membership of the profession have a clear view as to who benefits from the planning system, a view which is in stark distinction to that purveyed by the professional community of planning for consumption by society as a whole. Whereas the membership is clear that certain groups benefit (and presumably that other groups lose out), the profession, of necessity, portrays planning as an activity which benefits all groups in society equally, since it unarguably operates in the public interest. As was argued in Chapter 4, this position was a necessary element of professionalisation, and must be seen as an essential, publicly declared position if the occupational group of planning is to retain its privileged status.

These comments must be seen in the context of the fact that several respondents were at pains to emphasise a distinction between the 'is' and the 'ought', in that they accepted that certain social groups benefitted, but that they saw this as wrong and as a kind of malfunction of planning (rather than as a consequence of the distribution of power and income in society). Nevertheless, if the views expressed here are representative, and there is no reason to suppose that they are not, there is not much evidence of them being aired in any professional journals, papers or conferences. In other words, although planners might agree that certain groups benefit more than others, and perhaps even agree that this is wrong or unjust, these views do not seem to receive much of an airing within planning circles. The reasons for this are, of course, not known. However, it may be that since such views run contrary to the interests of the profession as a whole, and that the 'professional community' of planning is likely to be reluctant to encourage or support such views, individual members are dissuaded from promulgating them because such behaviour breaches the 'ground rules' of the profession which all members tacitly accept on entry. Hence, this can be seen as one way in which this expert labour force is subjected to a process of moral regulation.

Political attitudes

The Marcus and Knox and Cullen surveys both showed that planners had voting preference which were similar to those of the electorate as a whole. The findings of this survey, however, show that in mid-1990, most planners would have voted against the Conservative government, and that the party which attracted most support was the Labour Party (Table 5.13). Even amongst the private sector sample,where support for the Conservative Party might be expected to be highest, only 22% of the sample said that they would vote Tory if there were to be an election tomorrow. In contrast, 26% said that they would vote Labour, 12% Liberal Democrat and 6% Green.

Table 5.13
Voting intentions

If you were to vote in a General Election tomorrow, which would you vote for?

	Public sector		Private sector		All	
Labour Party	41.3%	(85)	26.6%	(13)	38.4%	(98)
Conservative Party	8.7%	(18)	22.4%	(11)	11.4%	(29)
Liberal Democrat	14.6%	(30)	12.2%	(6)	14.1%	(36)
Green Party	3.4%	(7)	6.1%	(3)	3.9%	(10)
Plaid Cymru	2.4%	(5)	0.0%	(0)	2.0%	(5)
Not Tory	1.5%	(3)	4.1%	(2)	2.0%	(5)
Not stated/don't know	28.1%	(58)	28.6%	(14)	28.2%	(72)
	100.0%	(206)	100.0%	(49)	100.0%	(255)

Whilst these private sector sample figures could be seen as an insignificant deviation from the national pattern (particularly bearing in mind the small sample), the figures for the public sector were more clearly weighted towards the Labour Party, with just over 40% of the respondents, whilst a mere 8.7% said that they would vote Conservative. Although the survey did not investigate the reasons for this pattern of preferences, it seems likely, given the responses to other questions, that the Conservative administrations of the 1980s are seen by many planners as having eroded the powers and significantly reduced the funding of both local government and the planning system during the decade. Moreover, many planners are likely to have taken the view that Thatcherism was ideologically committed to an anti-planning stance.

In contrast, it seems possible that many planners, particularly those in local government could support the Labour Party as representing a commitment to 'planning' in the widest sense (as opposed to the market), and a specific commitment to extend planning powers and local government if elected. These, as it were, professional, reasons for supporting Labour may well be more or less important than personal commitments extending over a long period of time, and the information produced by this survey does not shed any light on this. Neither is it possible to comment on whether or not planning attracts a particular kind of person with a particular political orientation - perhaps a general commitment to 'welfare', to 'serving the public' or even to helping the deprived and underprivileged. What is clear, however, is that at the time of the survey, this sample did not support the government and would not re-elect it.

The final part of the questionnaire asked the sample to respond to a series of normative statements by selecting one of the categories of strongly agree; agree; neither agree nor disagree; disagree; strongly disagree. The statements broadly refer to issues related to the work of town planners and were as follows:

> The privatisation of the gas, water and electricity industries is wrong.
>
> A strong and adequately funded 'welfare state' is an essential part of a modern democracy such as Britain.
>
> Governments should intervene in the housing market to ensure that dwellings are provided for those unable to afford owner-occupation.
>
> It is possible for a modern society to run effectively without the profit motive.
>
> Increases in commercial land values resulting from the granting of planning permission should be recouped through taxation.
>
> The problems of Britain's inner cities cannot be solved without massive public sector investment.

These attitudinal questions were put in order to judge how far the sample could be seen to be supportive of broadly capitalist perspectives as opposed to broadly socialist perspectives. It was not an attempt to replicate the survey undertaken by Wright (1985) in the United States, where he sought to use attitudinal questions to resolve class alignments within his Marxist class scheme. Rather it was a more modest attempt to evaluate the political perspectives of this particular occupational group in order to contribute towards the debate over class analysis considered in Chapter 2.

Table 5.14
Attitudinal questions - public sector respondents

	Strongly agree	Agree	Neither	Disagree	Strongly disagree
1) Privatisation is wrong	18.8% (37)	19.0% (40)	4.0% (8)	3.0% (6)	2.0% (5)
2) A strong welfare	27.0% (55)	19.0% (39)	2.0% (4)	1.0% (1)	0.0% (0)
3) Governments should intervene in housing	29.0% (60)	17.0% (34)	1.0% (2)	2.0% (2)	1.0% (1)
4) A modern society	2.0% (3)	7.0% (15)	4.0% (8)	30.0% (62)	4.0% (8)
5) Increases in land value should be recouped	15.0% (31)	20.0% (42)	5.0% (11)	6.0% (12)	1.0% (1)
6) Inner cities	13.0% (26)	27.0% (55)	3.0% (6)	5.0% (10)	1.0% (1)

Notes:
i) Percentages - raw numbers in brackets (206 respondents)
ii) See text for full questions
iii) Not all respondents answered all questions
iv) Figures have been rounded to the nearest percentage point

Table 5.15
Attitudinal questions - private sector respondents

	Strongly agree	Agree	Neither	Disagree	Strongly disagree
1) Privatisation is wrong	18.0% (9)	28.0% (14)	18.0% (9)	20.0% (10)	8.0% (4)
2) A strong welfare	24.0% (12)	62.0% (31)	2.0% (1)	2.0% (1)	4.0% (2)
3) Governments should intervene in housing	22.0% (11)	50.0% (25)	10.0% (5)	10.0% (5)	2.0% (1)
4) A modern society	4.0% (2)	10.0% (5)	4.0% (2)	50.0% (25)	28.0% (14)
5) Increases in land value should be recouped	2.0% (1)	20.0% (10)	14.0% (7)	22.0% (11)	14.0% (7)
6) Inner cities	12.0% (6)	48.0% (24)	6.0% (3)	24.0% (12)	2.0% (1)

Notes:
i) Percentages - raw numbers in brackets (49 respondents)
ii) See text for full questions
iii) Not all respondents answered all questions
iv) Figures have been rounded to the nearest percentage point

Tables 5.14 and 5.15 outline the responses to these questions, and although they must be treated with a degree of caution, a number of interesting points emerge. Perhaps the most striking point is that the majority of the public sector sample either agreed or strongly agreed with five of the six statements. Bearing in mind that these statements all reflected a broadly leftist position, this confirms the response to the earlier question concerning the voting intentions of this group. However, it is also important to recognise that these questions focused mainly on issues that have a direct bearing on the work environment of the planning profession, and that the adoption by government of policies directed towards achieving the ends implied by the statements would clearly result in an enhancement of planners' professional status. Nevertheless, it is clear that public sector planners are broadly supportive of what might be termed interventionist policies, for reasons of social justice, professional self interest, or both. In contrast however, the majority of public sector respondents disagreed with the proposition that a modern society could be run without the profit motive. Whether rejection of this statement constitutes an acceptance of one of the main pillars of capitalist social relations at this point in time is open to debate. However, it does indicate that this group of planners at least are still committed to the idea of a market, albeit conditionally. The response to these statements provided by the private sector sample were, as would be expected, less supportive. They tended to offer more responses in the 'disagree' and 'strongly disagree' categories. However, significant numbers were still broadly in favour of interventionist policies - over 70% thought that the state should intervene in housing, and over 80% supported the welfare state for example, although they were less enthusiastic over recouping betterment than their public sector colleagues.

It must be emphasised that these responses should be treated with caution, since they are only a partial reflection of the political views of the respondents. However, it seems reasonable to suggest that planners generally hold political views which are broadly left of centre in the context of contemporary British politics, and which include giving strong support to policies of state intervention at least in the general area of planning and the built environment. These findings clearly contradict those of Knox and Cullen who found that planners at the end of the 1970s held political views which were more widely dispersed across the political spectrum. Nevertheless, on the basis of the responses to this questionnaire, there does not seem to be much evidence to suggest that planners hold political views which are in any substantial way a threat to the state or to capitalist social relations. Certainly most planners would appear to prefer a return to a form of social democratic politics which would result in policies designed to increase state intervention, but this cannot be interpreted as being 'anti-capital'. These attitudes also support Lash and Urry's claim that the service class will tend to be attracted to social democratic politics, not least in this case for the very good reason that, as Chapter 4 demonstrated, such politics are deeply rooted in the very ideology of planning, and an adherence to them is, in professional and career terms, a very rational position for most planners.

This chapter has sought to consider and evaluate the position of planners as individual members of an occupational group located within the general category of the service class. The values and attitudes of planners and their access to and exploitation of assets has been considered with a view to assessing the membership of the profession, rather than the activity of planning or the view of the profession purveyed by the professional community of planning. This evaluation of planners will now be considered in the final chapter of this study in the context of the wider discussions of expert labour and class undertaken in previous chapters.

6 Conclusions

The previous chapters have sought to examine a range of ideas and evidence which can shed light on the position of town planners in contemporary Britain. Moreover, through a consideration of this occupational group, various propositions concerning professionalism and professionalisation, the regulation and exploitation of expertise and the importance of organisation assets have also been examined. In this final chapter these themes will be brought together in order to draw a series of conclusions relating to the planning profession, to the changing nature of 'planning' itself, and to those wider areas of sociological interest that were outlined in the Introduction.

Town planning and the 'corporatist bargain'

In his wide-ranging and powerful critique of British town and country planning, Reade (1987) argues that there is what he terms a 'corporatist bargain' in existence between the planning profession and the state. In exchange for economic security and an official definition of their role as 'important', planners are expected, argues Reade:

> to create the impression that the property industry *is* regulated, that the worst of its potentially anti-social excesses *are* kept in check, and that all land is put to its socially best use, rather than that which maximises private profit or promotes sectional interests. (1987, p.132).

This view is held, with varying degrees of sophistication, by many observers of British town planning, and this analysis is attractive not least in that it helps to explain planning's rapid professionalisation, despite the doubts expressed by many authors as to the profession's theoretical and intellectual integrity.

It is, however, a partial argument. Reade does not spell out how this corporatist bargain was brokered or struck, and nor does he suggest how it might be maintained. He assumes that 'corporatism' is somehow synonymous with 'incorporation' and that this involves a process whereby planners are somehow collectively brought within a governmental sphere of influence which ensures their compliance in exchange for privileges. By the same token, this position implies that occupational groups can act as cohesive bodies, somehow negotiating with 'the state'. As the discussions in previous chapters have indicated, although the planning profession may be viewed as participating in a corporatist relationship with the state, the nature of this relationship is likely to be more complex than Reade and others imply.

It was argued in Chapter 3 that the concept of corporatism, or more precisely liberal or neo-corporatism, refers specifically to a process of interest intermediation whereby interest organisations, whether they be the British Roads Federation or the Royal Town Planning Institute, have corporatist significance not as organisations representing their members' interests (although they undoubtedly do this) but in their role as intermediaries between their members and the state, in the sense that they have the capacity to regulate and control their membership in order to deliver agreed policy objectives. Corporatism as a model is thus applicable only when the state cannot directly intervene through authoritative regulation, but where it has to depend on others to achieve its ends. The state may therefore need to enter into corporatist mediation with trades unions or employers' federations in order to secure policy objectives in the economic sphere, or with professions in order to achieve welfare policy objectives.

This process of corporatist intermediation clearly involves two major elements. On the one hand, the state grants to interest organisations such as professions a high level of influence on policy matters in their respective areas. In exchange, the interest associations are expected to participate in achieving policy goals which fit within certain parameters and limits. Crucially, this means delivering the compliance of association members in the implementation of policy, since it is clear that no interest association will be permitted to participate in corporatist intermediation if it cannot demonstrate its capacity to perform this fundamental role.

Corporatism therefore involves making a distinction between 'the interest organisation' and 'the membership'. In the case of the welfare professions such as town planning, the process of corporatist intermediation means that the profession, (that is the professional institute or the small group of senior professionals who effectively control the Institute - in Laffin's (1986) terms, the 'professional community') must be seen as being distinct from the rank and file membership of the profession. It is not helpful to conflate the two as Reade and other observers have done in the case of the planning profession. Laffin's insights are particularly useful here as these permit a view of professions where the 'ground rules' for the membership in general and for the conduct of the professional area of responsibility are effectively set by the two groupings of the 'professional community' and the 'policy community'. Professional or 'expert' membership of the second group will largely be drawn from the first, and it is this second small grouping of the policy community which is likely to be the forum within which corporatist intermediation takes place. The professional community in turn, has the responsibility for delivering the compliance of the membership as a whole in the achievement of agreed policy objectives. Whilst it must be recognised that there is a danger of oversimplification in characterising corporatist intermediation in these terms, Laffin's conceptualisation enables a clearer view of how a 'corporatist bargain' might be operationalised.

This distinction within a profession between the membership and the professional community is an important and useful one. In the case of town planning there may be significant differences between the pronouncements of the professional community of planning, and the views of individual members as expressed in response to a confidential survey. Whilst, for example, the professional community of planning portrays the planning process as an activity which benefits all members of society, the rank and file membership have a very clear view that this is not the case, and that particular sections or actors benefit disproportionately. However, these inevitably heretical views tend not to be aired in any of the professional journals, conferences, meetings or papers. The reasons for this are, or course, unknown, but it seems likely that such views run counter to the interests of the profession as a whole, and that the professional community of planning is likely to be reluctant to encourage or support them, and individual members holding these views are going to be unwilling to promulgate them because such behaviour breaches the 'ground rules' of the profession which all members tacitly accept on entry. As with all social organisations, the regular breaching of codes, conventions and informal rules is likely to incur unofficial if not formal censure by professional colleagues, and possible exclusion from benefits such as promotion.

These ground rules for professional behaviour are a direct consequence of the position of the profession of town planning as a corporatist intermediary, and must be understood as a reflection of what constitutes legitimate knowledge within this professional domain. It has been argued in earlier chapters that the state legitimises credentials and professional knowledge. Appropriate or legitimate professional knowledge is thus likely to be deemed to be so by reference to the role that the particular profession plays in the process of corporatist intermediation. The welfare professions for example, claim to be able to solve social and economic problems within the pattern of existing social and economic relationships, and since this is in any event going to be a precondition for participation in corporatist intermediation, this in turn is likely to determine what constitutes legitimate knowledge, and in turn appropriate behaviour, in any particular professional sphere.

The existence of unwritten but clearly understood 'ground rules' in the planning profession, which indicate which beliefs and views are appropriate and acceptable for professional planners ensures that the professional community of planning can fulfil its corporatist obligation of securing the compliance of its members in the implementation of agreed policy. Most planners will know what these ground rules are, gleaned from their regular reading of the professional press, from their attendance at conferences and courses, from their regular contacts with professional colleagues and from the professional ethos which is likely to have been cultivated during their planning education. They will be well aware of which views and attitudes are likely to be judged 'legitimate' or perhaps 'reasonable', 'realistic' or 'achievable' by their peers, and those which will not be and will therefore breach the ground rules.

Of course, this is not to argue that this highly educated and presumably intelligent group of workers are somehow being duped or manipulated by the professional community of planning. Nor is to ignore the fact that many planners have deeply-held views of a humanitarian or politically radical nature which may run counter to the professional ethos of planning which has its expression in the professional ground rules discussed here. What is being suggested is that the profession of planning has, inevitably perhaps, become established as a corporatist intermediary in the process of state policy making in the area of land use and the built environment. In order to continue to influence policy in this area, and to continue to receive the benefits which flow from the recognition of planning as a legitimate profession, the professional community of planning must ensure that the membership of the Royal Town Planning Institute is seen to behave and perform in certain, acceptable, ways. Undoubtedly many, perhaps most, of the rank and file membership of the profession recognise the wisdom of this strategy, whether they perceive it in terms of self-interest (continued security of employment and job opportunities), or in the wider terms of securing a better world by keeping a seat for planning at the decision-making table. As Larson (1977) and Johnson (1972) have both pointed out, occupational groups can easily lose professional status, and it is clear from the survey results discussed in Chapter 5, that many planners recognise the potential fragility of their profession. The Institute itself has become acutely aware of this as the harmonisation of professional qualifications in Europe takes place. No other European country, with the possible exception of the Netherlands, has an established and nationally recognised profession dealing with land use and the built environment. Hence the concern expressed by the secretary of the RTPI at the news that in France, architects were seeking to undertake work which in Britain would be done by Institute members (Fryer, 1989; Shepley & Fryer, 1991).

Thus, Reade is correct in arguing the existence of a corporatist bargain between 'planning' and the state. However, he argues the case partially, ignoring the role of the Institute as a corporatist intermediary, and neglecting the important distinction to be made within the profession between the professional community and the membership. In addition he does not consider the mechanisms through which this process of corporatist intermediation unfolds - the policy community through which professionals and state representatives negotiate policy and determine what constitutes legitimate knowledge, and the professional community which has the responsibility for ensuring the compliance of the membership by maintaining appropriate ground rules for professional behaviour and belief. Hence, if professionalism is to be defined as one mode of moral regulation of expert labour (Crompton, 1990a), then, in the case of town planning at least, this must be regarded as an inevitable consequence of the process of corporatist intermediation, rather than as a reflection of collective self-regulation by an occupational group. The nature of this expert labour and the ways in which expertise can be exploited and controlled can now be examined.

Town planning, skills and expertise

As was pointed out in Chapter 3, experts are usually understood as people who have expertise in an area of 'legitimate' knowledge, that is, an area of knowledge that is sanctioned or approved by the state. However, as the discussion above makes clear, this does not necessarily mean that this expertise has universal credibility or status. If the criteria for the legitimation of knowledge is that such knowledge is useful to the state in the achievement of certain policy objectives, then it would not be surprising if certain individuals and groups in society rejected the validity of this knowledge or expertise, whilst others may well be completely indifferent to or ignorant of it. This is certainly true in the case of the cognitive competence or expertise claimed by planners. As has already been demonstrated, many writers, commentators, academics, politicians, journalists and community activists have consistently argued that the expertise claimed by planners is non-existent or irrelevant. Many have argued that the planners' function would be more effectively exercised by others, for example the residents, the people living in the localities to be planned. While this might be viewed as a naive and unrealistic position, it does emphasis the contention put by Abercrombie and Urry (1983) and others that knowledge and expertise must be understood as appropriated commodities - in this case the knowledge of how best to manage the residents' own local environment. By the same token, this point serves to illustrate Illich's (1977) claim that professions disable non-professionals through a somewhat similar process.

What is interesting about the particular case of planning however, is that it is reasonable to state that the planners themselves find it difficult to precisely identify the character of the expertise that they claim to hold. Moreover, as Healey and Underwood (1978) have argued, planners appear to have little in the way of particular expertise or skill, and, they conclude, planning knowledge appears to consist more of idealism and 'symbolic statements' than technical expertise. The review of planning and planners conducted in Chapters 4 and 5 would certainly support this conclusion.

Nevertheless, despite these difficulties, planners' established position as a professionalised occupational group reflects a successful claim to control over a cognitive base. In Abercrombie and Urry's terms, planners have been successful in appropriating knowledge away from the direct producers, since they have established the right to be regarded as experts in the field of land use and the built environment. This area clearly has many active participants - landowners, developers, residents, and so on, plus of course, the other professional occupations operating in the field such as architects and surveyors - all of whom may have extensive and valuable relevant knowledges. The planning profession however, has claimed epistemological prominence, legitimised by the state and supported by the systemisation and codification of planning knowledge through education and credentialisation. The issue of whether or not planning knowledge is worthwhile, valid or widely accepted is unimportant in this context. What is important is the capacity of a particular middle class occupational group not only to generate particular 'knowledge contents', but also to appropriate, embellish and utilise knowledge for its own ends. In the wider context of class analysis, Abercrombie and Urry (1983) argue that this therefore makes knowledge an axis of class formation, and this will be explored at the end of this chapter within the discussion of class.

Turning now to the organisation of expert labour within professions, Crompton's (1990a; 1990b) definition of professions as one mode of regulation of expert labour is particularly helpful. As was argued in Chapter 3, this definition permits an understanding of professions unencumbered by the largely ideological descriptions of the trait approach. Crompton, like Johnson (1972), argues that professionalism is a way of controlling or regulating an occupation, and that this control or regulation is exercised by the profession itself and demanded by the purchasers of those expert services. Thus, professional altruism may be viewed as a strategy to convince the public and purchasers that the profession operates in the public interest, although it will probably also reflect a genuine desire amongst professionals to ensure high ethical standards. The discussion that has been mounted in previous chapters and above suggests that there is a further dimension to this perception. The process of moral regulation of expert labour through the institutions of professions may, in the case of town planning at least, also be seen as part of the process of corporatist intermediation. The regulation of the expert labour of the membership of the Royal Town Planning Institute through adherence to the 'ground rules' of professional conduct and belief is in major part a reflection of the corporatist relationship that the planning profession has with the state. Professional ethics concerning relationships with the client (whoever that might be for public sector planners) are, in the case of the planning professional, clearly laid out in the Code of Professional Conduct. Such rules constitute regulation of members conduct and may be seen as formally fulfilling the objectives and purposes described by Crompton. What is being argued here is that in the case of town planning, the process of moral regulation of expert labour also operates in a more directly self-interested way in order to protect the long-term security of the profession. Whether this applies in other professions will have to be the subject of further enquiry, but it is likely that corporatist intermediation exists involving professions, particularly the welfare professions, in many sectors of public policy.

In reality of course, as has been argued earlier, most professional planners do not use much in the way of particular planning skills or expertise in their day to day work. Most are employed in large public sector organisations and are engaged in the processes of implementing state policy. This involves a wide range of skills and attributes concerning negotiation, inter-personal skills, knowledge of policy programmes, implementation skills and so on, but in general these are capacities and skills which would be expected from any well-educated and capable person. They are not, as Healey and Underwood (1978) point out, skills with a clear planning specificity or even technical intricacy. Thus, to use Larson's (1977) terminology, most planners, and certainly most senior planners are best regarded as technobureaucratic professionals as opposed to public service professionals. In other words, they tend to undertake tasks which involve carrying out the administrative and managerial functions associated with public policy. In contrast, public service professionals are those occupational categories which have emerged to service the functions of the modern state - teachers, social workers and housing managers for example. Town planners should, of course be included in this category, but as has been shown, an examination of their work demonstrates that only the most junior members of the profession operate in this way, that is carrying out specific expert tasks. It is clear that in professional work generally, the highest status is reserved for those positions exercising non-technical, interpersonal skills, and also, as individual professionals' careers unfold, they tend, in planning at least, to move away from technical, professional tasks towards more managerially oriented responsibilities.

Expert workers who fall into this technobureaucratic category, whether they are formally 'professionals' or not, may find that they are increasingly subject to a 'clan' form of regulation of expert labour (Crompton, 1990b). In the case of town planning this may be represented as a commitment to 'public service' or a sense of duty to the electorate. The survey outlined in Chapter 5 revealed a strong sense of loyalty to public service, and although the precise foundations of this are not known, it seems likely that this can and does exert a strong force of moral regulation amongst public employees in terms of duty, responsibility and obligation. The strength of this may be judged by the large number of respondents to the questionnaires who expressed a commitment to serving the public, despite the very difficult circumstances that many local government officers have operated under during recent years. In the particular case of town planners there is, of course, a convergence of belief and orientation between the professional ethos of planning and the notion of public service, and it must be recognised that this may not be so apparent in other professional areas such as accountancy or engineering. Nevertheless, it may well be that many expert workers are subjected to, and readily accept, moral regulation of their work practices through both their organisation of work and their professional institution.

This process of regulation of labour is to an extent mirrored by the categories of skill assets and organisation assets identified by Wright (1985). The wider significance of assets in the process of class analysis will be dealt with below, but at this juncture it is useful to comment on these categories in the light of town planning and the expertise that is exploited by planners. In the case of skill assets, the discussion above and in earlier chapters has sought to demonstrate that the skills and expertise claimed by the profession are in fact rather restricted. Nevertheless, town planners are a highly credentialised occupational group, and the profession has used its status as a corporatist intermediary to ensure firstly that 'planning' has maintained a prominent position in land use policy making and implementation, and thus that the career opportunities for town planners have not been too restricted, and secondly that the educational system has continued to provide ever more prestigious academic qualifications for professional planners. Thus, notwithstanding the apparent paucity of precise skills or even a coherent theoretical base, during the last two decades there has been a steady demand for people in possession of the appropriate planning qualifications. In this sense, individual planners may be exploiting credential assets rather than skill assets.

However, as was argued above, if most planners, and particularly most senior planners may be seen as technobureaucratic rather than public service professionals, it may well be that they are relying on organisation rather than skill assets for their prestige, status and material rewards at the individual level. This debate will be pursued below in the context of the asset approach to class analysis, but at this point it is necessary on the basis of this examination of town planners, to underscore the importance of credentials rather than skills in the context of expert labour. It is the public declaration of the individual's possession of legitimate knowledge which is important, which in turn may well be a consequence of her particular profession's position as a corporatist intermediary. This in itself is in turn a recognition of the importance of that particular policy area to the state.

The 'value' or marketability of the particular skills which the individual expert has to offer may be secondary in this context to the structures of career and credentials which have in large part been established by the actions of the profession acting in its role as a corporatist intermediary. All this applies to town planning, and it may well be that other expert and credentialed occupations cannot be assessed in the same terms, but as studies of housing management and traffic engineering show (Laffin, 1986), these occupations exhibit similar characteristics, and there is no obvious reason why other welfare professions such as social work should not be expected to do the same. In short, skill assets may in many cases be credential assets, and these in turn are valuable not for any intrinsic reason but because a market for them has been created by the profession concerned. The fact that other countries seem to manage perfectly well without certain professional groups and their associated career structure and expertise well illustrates the point. In France, for example there is no equivalent profession to that of general practice surveyor, who form the bulk of the membership of the Royal Institution of Chartered Surveyors in Britain, and, as has been mentioned above, there is no profession of town planning performing the function that RTPI members perform in the U.K. Thus although it is reasonable to point out that many experts perform important and necessary tasks which are essential to the effective running of a society, it is equally important to recognise that this is not a universal axiom.

Finally, it is also important to emphasise that possession of credentials gives access to control over technical knowledge and information, and this is of course particularly true of public sector workers such as planners. As the discussion in Chapter 3 has emphasised, this control may permit significant influence over policy making and implementation which, although it may not benefit particular individuals, may reap rewards for groupings such as the professional occupation as a whole, workers employed within the organisation, or even 'the middle class' generally.

The 'asset approach' to class analysis

How useful is the asset approach to class analysis? It is certainly clear that the concepts of skills assets and organisation assets have proved useful as heuristic devices for understanding town planners. However, what light can be shed on the character of the assets themselves?

Wright and Savage *et al.* view organisation assets principally as rewards accruing to the individual as a consequence of bureaucratic position. The controllers of such assets are able to manipulate organisations in order to, for example further their own careers, or perhaps to use their influence within the organisation to achieve advantageous consequences for themselves, friends or family. However, this is a partial view of organisation assets. Although these processes undoubtedly take place, it is extremely difficult to identify and quantify them since they take place at the level of the individual and may even involve illegal practices. In defining organisation assets in this way Wright seems to have in mind the situation which has existed in bureaucratically controlled communist societies, where it might until recently have been possible to argue that there was wide exploitation of organisation assets undertaken by public officials to achieve these kind of personal gains.

However, in the context of Britain such a definition ignores the possibility that the control of such assets might result in benefits for whole sections of the population rather than for specific individuals. This leads to a definition of organisation assets as mechanisms which may be manipulated, explicitly or implicitly, in order to ensure that the organisation's resources or actions benefit particular broad social groups in society, usually the middle or service class. This manipulation is not likely to occur as a conscious or premeditated act. Rather, it will be the cumulative result of a series of decisions and actions which are individually 'rational' in that they reflect the rationality of the decision makers and those that influence them. Organisation assets can only be exploited by the controllers or holders of asset-controlling mechanisms while such people are employed by the organisation. When they leave the organisation what they are effectively doing is taking with them organisational knowledge. They are trading in organisation assets for economic assets via, to use Wright's conceptualisation, skill assets.

Similar problems arise with skill assets. This discussion above and in earlier chapters has been concerned to argue that it is credentials and not skills that are important. Undoubtedly there are individuals who possess certain uncredentialed skills which can be sold on the market in the same way that manual crafts people - plumbers, carpenters, upholsterers - sell their skills. However, the central point about service class occupations is that they involve the expropriation and codification of knowledge, normally in the form of extended education and credentials. It is the possession and exploitation of the credentials which is the asset - regardless of any judgement as to their real value - rather than some less tangible notion of 'skill'. Wright objects that credentials only have significance if they are exploited. However, this is true of all assets, including economic assets. Mere possession is not enough - the asset must be actively exploited.

It seems likely that service class members may use a combination of assets in order to reap material benefits for themselves, and it is not immediately apparent that groups based on public - private sector or a large organisation - small organisation divide can realistically be seen to comprise individuals who principally exploit one asset rather than another. Certainly, the case of town planning does not easily fit into this framework. The profession has clearly established itself on the basis of its exercise of skill in the 'science and art of town planning', and it has laid successful claim to a cognitive competence. Most planners are employed in the public sector, but their very presence there is a consequence of their claim to exercise skills. Moreover, if at any time this claim was dropped, the planning profession would become extremely vulnerable. In this sense planners are exploiting skill or rather credential assets, instead of organisation assets.

In the case of the planners in the private sector, virtually all of whom work for small organisations, the situation is somewhat similar. The main difference here is that such planners have, in varying degrees, cashed in their organisational experience for economic assets. They are no longer controlling organisation assets as defined above, but they are still likely to be benefitting from them by virtue of their position as members of the middle or service class. After all, as Chapter 5 demonstrated, planners are clear in their view that the articulate middle class and property owners are the main beneficiaries of the planning process, that is of the decisions made by the controllers of organisation assets.

The position of planners in a relatively well paid and secure occupation is due principally to their control and exploitation of expert knowledge. The tangible asset held by planners is credentials, not skills, and it is these credentials, principally membership of the Royal Town Planning Institute, which enables individual planners to secure their position. However, although planners in the public and private sector earn reasonable salaries, these are not in any way spectacular, and they are likely to be equalled by a significant number of skilled manual and intermediate white collar occupations. In this sense at least, the asset of credentials is not a remarkably powerful one. Nevertheless, when household income and economic assets such as shares and property are examined, planners begin to look more prosperous.

In part this must be due to circumstances which were not considered by the survey undertaken here, the most obvious being the consequences of capital appreciation through home ownership and the benefits of inheritance, both of which are likely sources of capital acquisition common to middle class groups. However, what is clear is that about 70% of planners surveyed were members of households with more than one earner and that the majority of these households had incomes in excess of £35,000 per annum. It is possible that the increase in employment opportunities for credentialed women results in more dual income households with a substantial total earnings. Thus, although the sample could be considered as relatively prosperous and in possession of considerable economic assets, it seems probable that this is in part a consequence of changing employment patterns and perhaps also a result of inheritance, rather than being simply the result of the exploitation of skill or credential assets.

Turning now to the wider notion of cultural capital - which could legitimately incorporate credential assets - it seems clear that planners, like other middle class people are knowledgable, articulate and capable. They can, as planners themselves recognise, have a great deal of influence on the decision- making process in planning as objectors, local residents, environmentalists and so on. The capacity to secure benefits for one's own locality or environment is as much a consequence of cultural capital as ensuring that one's children succeed in the educational system.

Much of the discussion on assets and class to date has tended to focus upon the employment position of individual members of the middle class. Although this is clearly important, what is being suggested here is that these assets will also have significance, often quite considerable significance outside of the workplace. Members of the service class and of the middle class generally will utilise cultural capital, organisation assets and economic assets to secure and maintain their privileged position over other classes by actions outside of the workplace as well as by actions within. Credential assets as part of the wider notion of cultural capital, are likely to have leverage primarily, though not exclusively within the world of work. Organisation assets defined either in Wright's terms or in the wider sense suggested above, will be exploited at the work place, although their consequences will probably range considerably wider. Cultural capital, in the wider sense employed by Bourdieu and others is surely much more generally distributed amongst the middle class and the service class than has often been suggested. Although it might be reasonable to suggest that public sector workers rely heavily upon cultural capital (probably mainly in the form of credential assets) to secure advantages in the employment market, it seems likely that in the wider arena of political and social activity many middle class members utilise this asset in order to secure and maintain their real income and lifestyle.

Town planners, the middle class and the service class

Although the survey discussed in Chapter 5 indicated that many town planners do not think of themselves as belonging to any particular social class, it is quite clear that on virtually every taxonomy of occupations, they would be assigned to the middle class or some similar designation. However, in the context of the contemporary debate over class, it is more interesting to consider how far this occupational group exhibit the characteristics of the putative service class. It was argued in Chapter 2, that Goldthorpe's conception of the service class is less helpful than that of Urry and his colleagues in terms of understanding how particular occupational groups located between capital and labour are likely to relate to these two. Thus, the discussion below seeks to re-assess this particular notion of the service class in the light of the evidence gathered in previous chapters relating to one particular service class occupation.

This first problem however, is that Lash and Urry's (1987) definition of the service class seems to exclude occupations such as town planning. As was mentioned in Chapter 2, the contention that the service class refers to places located within a set of institutions that 'service' capital by conceptualising the labour process, by controlling the entry and exercise of labour power within the workplace and by orchestrating the non-household forms under which labour power is produced and regulated, results in a definition which ignores a wide range of occupations (Crompton 1990a). There is no explanation of why this is so, and nothing in their work which would suggest that this is anything other than a consequence of Lash and Urry's tendency "to discuss industrial management as a proxy for the 'service class' as a whole" (Crompton 1990a, p.7), On the contrary, it has been argued above that the profession of town planning exists principally because of the services that it performs for the state. Moreover, it is clear that the major beneficiaries of the process of planning are the owners of land and property. Given these circumstances and the fact that this occupation fits every criteria set by Lash and Urry for inclusion into the service class, for example in terms of remuneration, career structure, the utilisation of credentials, the development of rational decision-making and so on, it would seem reasonable to categorise planning as a service class occupation.

However, how far does the examination of the profession of planning undertaken here support Lash and Urry's view of the service class? In large part their contentions are borne out, particularly with respect to the significance of credentials, the appropriation of knowledge and the importance of the expansion of professional and managerial occupations within the state in Britain during the post war period. However, there are a number of quite important points which are less clear. Central to Lash and Urry's view of the service class is the contention that this class was generated in the context of 'organised capital', where it grew out of the relationship with capital and labour. However, once it attained a certain level of development, argue Lash and Urry, this new class begins to have a disorganising effect on capitalist society. The service class is based primarily upon the control of knowledge and the possession of credentials, and Lash and Urry argue that this means that this class serves capital, but that it increasingly does so on its own terms - thus disorganising rather than organising capital.

However, the discussion of town planning above does not support this contention. It has been shown that the knowledge or expertise that planners possess exists principally because the state permits its existence and this, after all is the basis of legitimate knowledge. It is difficult to see how planners are increasingly serving capital on their own terms when the terms for the conduct of professional planning activity have been overwhelmingly set by the state and the market place. On the basis of the review carried out here, there does not appear to be much evidence of 'disorganising' tendencies. On the contrary, the planning profession seems geared up to preserve the status quo and keep the ship of land use on an even keel. In part this may be seen as a consequence of a survival strategy adopted by a reformist profession threatened by a radical free-market government during the last decade, but it seems equally likely that this is due to the profession's long term position as a corporatist intermediary.

By the same token, members of the profession due not hold views which can be judged as 'anti-capital'. The responses to the attitude questions discussed in Chapter 5 demonstrate clearly that, although planners may hold liberal views on some issues, in the main they are broadly supportive of policies and attitudes which maintain the status quo. There is little evidence to support the view that planners as an occupational group in any way constitute a threat to capital. On the contrary, all the evidence suggests that their objective interests are largely, though not completely, co-terminus with those of capital.

It might be objected that these comments apply to one, unrepresentative, occupational group, and that an examination of other groups would confirm Lash and Urry's contention that the service class is likely to be a disorganising force in a contemporary capitalism and that the oppositional grouping to capital from within the service class is "exceedingly large" (Lash and Urry, 1988 p.195). However, as Lash and Urry point out, the British service class is very much dominated by the development of the 'welfare state' and the associated professions and managerial occupations, of which town planning is an obvious and typical example. It may well be that other occupational groups within and closely associated with the public sector, and in particular those with 'professional' status, may exhibit similar characteristics to planners as a consequence of the imperatives of corporatist intermediation.

The concept of the service class as developed by Abercrombie and Urry and Lash and Urry has proved a useful heuristic device in examining town planners in that it has assisted in achieving an understanding and evaluation of this occupational group in terms of its relationship to other social groups, to the state and to major interests such as land and property. However, to what extent can the service class be understood as a class in terms of a collective identity or class consciousness? Is there any evidence of the chain of social action that Pahl refers to as the Structure-Consciousness-Action 'mantra' (Pahl, 1989)? On the basis of this short study, the answer to this must be 'no'. Town planners as an occupational group do not appear to exhibit characteristics which might be interpreted as constituting any degree of commonality of political interest or purpose. On the contrary, they are a comparatively disparate group in these terms. Any shared interest or commonality appears to derive principally from occupational interest rather than from any conception of class position.

On the basis of the evidence considered here, it is reasonable to conclude that planners' attitudes and values are generally supportive of capitalist social relations in the sense that most planners appear to accept the legitimacy of the market, albeit conditionally in many cases, and they are in the main supportive of the status quo. Although they may have reservations about the way in which developers and landed interests benefit from the planning system, these are not significant enough to prompt any major dissent. By the same token, although some planners nod in the direction of the interests of the 'deprived' or the 'underprivileged', these do not appear to be widely held attitudes, and again they do not appear to be supported by publicly expressed views.

In a sense, this is not surprising, since as has been exhaustively argued above, the interests of the profession and the interests of the state are mainly co-terminus, and the processes of moral regulation via professional ground rules tend to discourage dissent. However it does seem clear that, in the case of this occupational group at least, there is little support for Renner's view of the proletarianisation of the service class nor for Lash and Urry's contention that they are likely to constitute a disorganising force for capitalism. On the contrary, for planners at least, the reverse seems to be the case in both instances.

These attitudes and values are, as has been indicated above, a consequence of occupational commonality, something which has a long and detailed tradition within sociology, usually in the context of working class occupations (*e.g.* Dennis, Henriques and Slaughter, 1956), although of course, the concomitant class consciousness is absent in this case. Planners' views seem to be conditioned more by occupation than by class, and it may well be that a more useful way of understanding a concept such as 'the service class' is to accept that it is a collectivity of occupations rather than individuals. As several writers have noted, it is important to recognise the varied meanings of the concept of class, As Crompton suggests, it may be important to:

> be sensitive to the fact that some approaches, and some measures, may be more useful for some problems, and in some analyses, than others, and that 'class' itself has a varying impact that changes over time, and is more salient in some situations than others. (Crompton, 1991, p.113).

In the context of the service class, it is suggested that this concept has utility as a mechanism for understanding the ways in which certain occupational groups employing 'educated labour' have managed to secure privileged positions over other groups and classes, and for helping to explain the ways in which these occupational groups may relate to other social classes and institutions, particularly the state. Each occupation may have different conditions and circumstances which may only be understood by examining that occupation or profession in the way that has been undertaken here, and it would be interesting to discover if other service class occupations exhibit similar characteristics to planning. The emphasis though, should be on occupations rather than individuals since the concept of the service class is defined by these.

Individuals not in employment are by definition excluded from the concept as of course, are non-service class occupations. Thus, the service class cannot be an all-embracing concept which may be seen as a proxy for the 'middle class'. Rather it should be understood as a tool for unlocking insights into certain sections of the middle class.

By the same token, the 'asset approach' offers insights into the processes of class formation in the case of the middle class, bearing in mind the reservations expressed above over the nature of organisation and skill assets. On the basis of a study of one section of expert labour it certainly appears that these assets are tangible and transferable into economic assets and vice versa. Moreover, it is equally clear that, given a suitable social, economic and political environment, these assets can be generated and reproduced by politically competent and powerful groups. In this sense, as Abercrombie and Urry argue, knowledge is an axis of class formation, although it may well be that class action will only materialise when this very axis of knowledge, and the associated structures of professionalism and credentialisation are threatened.

Town planning, politics and professionalism

The emphasis throughout this book has been upon the profession of planning and the analysis of the planners themselves as representatives of the credentialised, expert labour force. But what of 'planning'? All developed societies require some mechanism for allocating land use in the built and natural environments and for deciding upon the 'best' and most suitable forms of development. In Britain, the profession of planning has established itself as expert in these matters, and has played a central role in the creation of a system of land use control which portrays as 'technical' decisions which are largely political. It is a testament to the power of educated labour that it has been possible to construct a profession on the basis of such shaky epistemological grounds. As has been seen, 'planning' has been more about 'symbolic statements' than expertise.

Much of the criticism which was directed at planning during the 1960s and 1970s, centred on the credibility of planners' expertise. It was regularly argued that the 'planners' were no more expert than the people for whom they were planning. Undoubtedly, the retreat during the 1980s into a more regulatory, semi-judicial form of planning, has blunted this criticism, but this has been replaced by a concern as to the apparent inability of the planning profession to control or regulate the worst excesses of the property development industry during the boom years. As a profession, planning is high profile and potentially vulnerable, as are some other welfare professions - social work springs to mind for example. But planning has created expectations which it has been unable to meet, and in major part this is a direct consequence of its cognitive base and the drive for professional status. When 'planning' abandoned its early social movement roots and sought professional status, when it began to appropriate knowledge from other professionals and 'ordinary people' in order to establish its legitimate cognitive base, it also abandoned politics, at least in the sense of public discussion and debate and the search for political support. This move away from politics, from the charismatic reformers of the early part of this century to the routinised planning of the 1980s and 1990s is a classically Weberian process.

The pattern of land use in Britain is decided primarily by the market and not by planning, and it is equally clear that the planners themselves know this, despite the Royal Town Planning Institute's refusal to countenance such heresy. The issues that planners concern themselves with are real and important, in that they affect the day to day lives and futures of millions of people and their children. However, 'planning' will be unable to unlock its potential for addressing these problems in any serious way until it begins to rediscover politics. And the cost of doing this of course, is the loss of professional and expert status.

Bibliography

ABERCROMBIE, N. & URRY, J., (1983), *Capital, Labour and the Middle Classes*, London, Allen and Unwin.

ADAM SMITH INSTITUTE, (1983), *Omega Report: Local Government Policy*, London, Adam Smith Institute

AGYEMAN, J. & EVANS, B., (eds.), (1994), *Local Environmental Policies and Strategies*, Harlow, Longman.

ALBROW, M., (1970), *Bureaucracy*, London, MacMillan.

ALBRECHTS, L., (1991), 'Changing Roles and Positions of Planners', in *Urban Studies*, vol.28, no.1, pp.123-137.

AMBROSE, P., (1986), *Whatever Happened to Planning?*, London, Methuen.

ANTHIAS, K., (1990), 'Race and class revisited - conceptualising race and racisms', *Sociological Review*, Jan/Feb 1990.

ASHWORTH, W., (1954), *The Genesis of Modern British Town Planning*, London, Routledge and Kegan Paul.

BACHRACH, P. & BARATZ, M.S., (1963), 'Decisions and Non-decisions: an Analytical Framework', *American Political Science Review*, 57.

BAGGULEY, P., MARK-LAWSON, J., SHAPIRO, D., URRY, J., WALBY, S. & WARDE, A., (1990), *Restructuring: Place, Class and Gender*, London, Sage.

BAILEY, J., (1975), *Social Theory and Planning*, London, Routledge and Kegan Paul.

BAILEY, J., (1980), *Ideas and Intervention: Social Theory for Practice*, London, Routledge and Kegan Paul.

BALL, M., (1983), *Housing Policy and Economic Power: The Political Economy of Owner-Occupation*, London, Methuen.

BARBALET, J.M., (1986), 'Limitations of class theory and the disappearance of status: the problem of the new middle class', *Sociology*, vol.20, no.4, pp.557-75.
BARRETT, S. & FUDGE, C., (eds.), (1981), *Policy and Action*, London, Methuen.
BARLOW, (1940), *Report of the Royal Commission on the Distribution of the Industrial Population*, London, HMSO.
BELL, D., (1976), *The Coming of Post-Industrial Society*, New York, Basic Books.
BACKWELL, J. & DICKENS, P., (1978), *Town Planning, Mass Loyalty and the Reconstruction of Capital: The Origins of the 1947 Planning Legislation Revisited*, University of Sussex, Urban and Regional Studies Working Paper, no.11.
BLOWERS, A., (1980), *The Limits of Power: The Politics of Local Planning Policy*, Oxford, Pergamon.
BLOWERS, A., (ed.), (1993), *Planning for a Sustainable Environment*, London, Earthscan.
BOADEN, N., GOLDSMITH, M., HAMPTON, W. & STRINGER, P., (1982), *Public Participation in Local Services*, Harlow, Longman.
BOTTOMORE, T. & BRYM, R., (1989), *The Capitalist Class: an International Study*, New York, Harvester Wheatsheaf.
BOURDIEU, P., (1984), *Distinction: a Social Critique of the Judgement of Taste*, London, Routledge and Kegan Paul.
BOURDIEU, P., (1988), *Homo Academicus*, Cambridge, Polity.
BRAVERMAN, H., (1974), *Labour and Monopoly Capital: The Degradation of Work in the Twentieth Century*, New York, Monthly Review Press.
BRINDLEY, T., RYDIN, Y. & STOKER, G., (1989), *Remaking Planning: The Politics of Urban Change in the Thatcher Years*, London, Unwin Hyman.
BRION, M. & TINKER, A., (1980), *Women in Housing: Access and Influence*, London, Housing Centre Trust.
BROADBENT, A., (1972), *Planning and Profit in the Urban Economy*, London, Methuen.
BROWN, R. & ELTIS, W., (1978), *Britain's Economic Problems: Two Few Producers*, London, Methuen.
BROWNHILL, S, (1990), *Developing London's Docklands. Another Great Planning Disaster?*, London, Paul Chapman.
BRUTON, M.J., (ed.), (1984), *The Spirit and Purpose of Planning*, (Second Edition), London, Hutchinson.
BULMER, M, (1986), *Neighbours: The Work of Philip Abrams*, Cambridge, Cambridge University Press.

BURRIS, V., (1989), 'New Directions in Class Analysis', *in* WRIGHT, 1989.
CARCHEDI, G., (1989), 'Classes and Class Analysis' *in* WRIGHT, 1989.
CARTER, B., (1985), *Capitalism, Class Conflict and the New Middle Class*, London, Routledge.
CASTELLS, R., (1977), *The Urban Question*, London, Arnold.
CHERRY, G.E., (1974), *The Evolution of British Town Planning*, London, Leonard Hill.
CHERRY, G., (1982), *The Politics of Town Planning*, Harlow, Longman.
CHERRY, G.E., (ed.), (1987), *Pioneers in British Planning*, London, Architecture Press.
CHERRY, G., (1991), 'Today's Issues in a 20th Century Perspective', *The Planner*, vol.77, no.1.
CLEGG, S. & DUNKERLEY, D., (1980), *Organisation, Class and Control*, London, Routledge.
CLOKE, P. & THRIFT, N., (1990), 'Class and Change in Rural Britain', *in* MARSDEN, *et al.*, 1990.
COLENUTT, B., (1990), *Politics not Partnership*, *in* MONTGOMERY, J. & THORNLEY, A., 1990.
COOKE, P., (1989), *Localities: The Changing Face of Urban Britain*, London, Unwin Hyman.
COOKE, P., (1983), *Theories of Planning and Spatial Development*, London, Hutchinson.
COOPER, A., (1984), 'Employment Survey of Branch Members: A Research Project for the RTPI East of England Branch', London, RTPI.
COWAN, P., (ed.), (1973), *The Future of Planning*, London, Heineman.
CRAIG, C., (1963), *The Employment of Cambridge Graduates*, Cambridge, Cambridge University Press.
CRICK, B., (1964), *In Defence of Politics*, Harmondsworth, Pelican.
CROMPTON, R. & GUBBAY, J., (1977), *Economy and Class Structure*, London, MacMillan.
CROMPTON, R. & JONES, G., (1984), *White Collar Proletariat*, London, MacMillan.
CROMPTON, R. & SANDERSON, K., (1986), 'Credentials and Careers: some implications of the increase in professional qualifications amongst women', *Sociology*, vol.20, no.1, pp.25-42.
CROMPTON, R., (1990a), 'Professions and the Service Class', Paper presented to the British Sociological Association Conference: Social Divisions and Social Change, Guildford, University of Surrey.
CROMPTON, R., (1990b), 'Professions in the Current Context', *Work, Employment and Society*, British Sociological Association, Special Issue, pp.147-166.

CROMPTON, R. & SANDERSON, K., (1990c), *Gendered Jobs and Social Change*, London, Unwin Hyman.
CROMPTON, R., (1991), 'Three Varieties of Class Analysis: comment on R.E. Pahl', *International Journal of Urban and Regional Research*, no.15, pp.108-113.
CULLINGWORTH, J.B., (1988), *Town and Country Planning in Britain*, (Tenth Edition), London, Unwin Hyman.
CULLINGWORTH, J.B., (1980), *Environmental Planning 1939-1969*, Volume IV: Land Values, Compensation and Betterment, London, HMSO.
DAHRENDORF, R., (1969), 'The Service Class', *in* BURNS, T., (ed.), *Industrial Man*, Harmondsworth, Penguin.
DAVIES, J.G., (1972), *The Evangelistic Bureaucrat*, London, Tavistock.
DEAR, M. & SCOTT, A.J., (1981), *Urbanization and Urban Planning in Capitalist Society*, London, Methuen.
DEARLOVE, J., (1973 *The Politics of Policy in Local Government*, Cambridge, Cambridge University Press.
DENNIS, N., (1956), HENRIQUES, F. & SLAUGHTER, C., *Coal is our Life*, London, Eyre and Spottiswoode.
DENNIS, N., (1972), *Public Participation and Planners' Blight*, London, Faber.
DEPARTMENT OF THE ENVIRONMENT, (1989), *Planning Control in Western Europe*, London, HMSO.
DICKENS, P., (1988), *One Nation? Social Change and the Politics of Locality*, London, Pluto.
DICKENS, P., (1990), *Urban Sociology: Society, Locality and Human Nature*, Hemel Hempstead, Harvester Wheatsheaf.
DINGWALL, R., & LEWIS, P., (1983), *The Sociology of Professions*, London, MacMillan.
DIRECTORY OF OFFICIAL ARCHITECTURE AND PLANNING, (1990), Harlow, Longman.
DUNCAN, S., & GOODWIN, M., (1988), *The Local State and Uneven Development*, Cambridge, Polity.
DUNLEAVY, P., (1980), *The Political Implications of Sectural Clearages and the Growth of State Employment*, Political Studies 28, pp. 364-83, 527-49.
DUNLEAVEY, P., (1981), *The Politics of Mass Housing in Britain 1945-75: A Study of Corporate Power and Professional Influence in the Welfare State*, Oxford, Clarendon.
DUNLEAVY, P., (1980), *Urban Political Analysis*, London, MacMillan.
DUNLEAVY, P., & HUSBANDS, C., (1986), *Democracy at the Crossroads*, London, Allen & Unwin.

DUNLEAVY, P., (1987), 'Professions and Policy Change: notes towards a model of ideological corporatism', *Public Administration Bulletin*, no.36, August.

EHRENREICH, B. & EHRENREICH, J., (1979), 'The Professional - Managerial Class', *in* WALKER, P., (ed.), 1979.

EHRMAN, R., (1988), *Planning Planning*, London, Centre for Policy Studies.

ELSON, M., (1986), *Green Belts: Conflict Mediation in the Urban Fringe*, London, Heineman.

EVANS, B., (1993), 'Why we no longer need a town planning profession', *Planning Practice and Research*, Vol.8, No.1.

EVANS, B., (1994), 'Theory, sustainability and environmental planning', *Town and Country Planning*, Vol.63, No.6.

EVERSLEY, D., (1973), *The Planner in Society: the changing role of a profession*, London, Faber and Faber.

FALUDI, A., (ed.), (1973), *A Reader in Planning Theory*, Oxford, Pergamon.

FOLEY, D., (1960), 'British Town Planning: one ideology or three?', *British Journal of Sociology*, vol.11, pp.211-31, also *in* FALUDI, A., (ed.), 1973.

FREIDSON, E., (ed.), (1973), *The Professions and Their Prospects*, London, Sage.

FREIDSON, E., (1983), 'The Theory of Professions: State of the Art', *in* DINGWALL, R. & LEWIS, P., 1983.

FRIEND, J.K. & JESSOP, W.N., (1969), *Local Government and Strategic Choice*, London, Tavistock.

FRYER, D., (1989), *The European Council of Town Planners; 1991, 1992 and then ...?*, Paper presented to the AESOP COnference, Durtmund, May, 1989.

GERTH, H. & MILLS, C.W., (1948), *From Max Weber*, London, Routledge and Kegan Paul.

GLASS, R., (1973), 'The Evaluation of Town Planning: Some Sociological Considerations', *in* FALUDI, A., 1973. (First published in *International Social Science Journal*, vol.XI, no.3, 1959).

GOLDTHORPE, J., (1982), 'On the Service Class, its formation and future', *in* GIDDENS, A. & MacKENZIE, G., (eds.), *Social Class and the Division of Labour*, Cambridge, Cambridge University Press.

GOLDTHORPE, J., (with LLEWELLYN, C. & PAYNE, C.,), (1987), *Social Mobility and Class Structure in Modern Britain*, Oxford, Clarendon (second edition).

GOULDNER, A., (1979), *The Future of Intellectuals and the Rise of the New Class*, New York, The Seabury Press.

GORZ, A., (1982), *Farewell to the Working Class*, London, Pluto Press.
GOULD, A., (1981), 'The Salaried Middle Class in the Corporatist Welfare State', *Policy and Politics*, vol.9, no.4, pp.401-418.
GRANT, W., (ed.), (1985), *The Political Economy of Corporatism*, Basingstoke, MacMillan.
GREED, C., (1991), *Surveying Sisters: Women in a Traditional Male Profession*, London, Routledge.
GREED, C., (1993), *Woment and Planning: creating gendered realities*, London, Routledge.
GREENWOOD, E., (1965), 'Attitudes of a Profession', *in* SALD, M., (ed.), *Social Welfare Institutions*, New York, Wiley.
GRIFFITHS, R. & AMOOQUAYE, E., (1989), 'The Place of Race in the Town Planning Agenda', *Planning Practice and Research*, vol.4, no.1.
GYFORD, J., LEACH. S., & GAME, C., (1989 *The Changing Politics of Local Government*, London, Unwin Hyman.
HAGUE, C., (1984), *The Development of Planning Thought: A Critical Perspective*, London, Hutchinson.
HALL, P., THOMAS, R., GRACEY, G. & DREWETT, R., (1973), *The Containment of Urban England*, (Two Volumes), London, Allen and Unwin.
HALL, P., (1989a), *Planning for a Golden Age*, The Planner, July 1989.
HALL, P., (1989b), *Urban and Regional Planning*, (Second Edition), London, Unwin Hyman.
HALL, P., (1989c), *London 2001*, London, Unwin Hyman.
HAM, C. & HILL, M., (1984), *The Policy Process in the Modern Capitalist State*, Brighton, Wheatsheaf.
HARDY, D., (1990), 'Consensus Planning: Realistic Goal or Idle Dream', *Planning Practice and Research*, vol.5, no.2.
HARVEY, D., (1973), *Social Justice and the City*, London, Edward Arnold.
HEALEY, P. & UNDERWOOD, J., (1978), 'Professional Ideals and Planning Practice: A Report on Research into Planners' Ideas in Practice in London Borough Planning Departments', *Progress in Planning*, vol.9, pp.73-127, Pergamon.
HEALEY, P., MCDOUGALL, G., & THOMAS, M J., (1982), *Planning Theory: Prospects for the 1980s*, Oxford, Pergamon.
HEALEY, P., (1983), *Local Plans in British Land-Use Planning*, Oxford, Pergamon.
HEALEY, P., (1985), 'The Professionalisation of Planning in Britain: Its Form and Consequences', *Town Planning Review*, 56(4).
HEALEY, P., McNAMARA, P., ELSON, N. & DOAK, A.J., (1989a), *Land-Use Planning and the Mediation of Urban Change*, Cambridge, Cambridge University Press.

HEALEY, P., (1989b), *Planning for the 1990s*, Working Paper no.7, Department of Town and Country Planning, University of Newcastle.
HEALEY, P., (1990), 'Democracy in the Planning System', *The Planner*, vol.76, no.19, pp.14-15.
HEARN, J., (1982), 'Notes on Patriarchy, Professionalism and the Semi-professions', *Sociology*, vol.16, no.2, pp.184-202.
HEATH, A., (1991), *Understanding Political Change: The British Voter 1964-1987*, London, Pergamon.
HINDESS, B., (1987), *Politics and Class Analysis*, Oxford, Blackwell.
HOWE, E. & KAUFMAN, J., (1979), 'The Ethics of Contemporary American Planners', *Journal of the American Planning Association*, vol.45, pp.243-255.
ILLICH, I., *et al.*, (1977), *Disabling Professions*, London, Marion Boyars.
JAMES, R., (1980), *Return to Reason: Popper's Thought in Public Life*, Shepton Mallet, Open Books.
JANWOITZ, M. & KASARDA, J.D., (1974), 'The Social Construction of Local Communities', *in* LEGGATT, T., (ed.), *Sociological Theory and Survey Research*, London, Sage.
JOHNSON, T.J., (1972 *Professions and Power*, Basingstoke, MacMillan.
JOHNSON, T.J., (1977 'The Professions in the Class Structure', *in* SCASE, R., 1977.
JOHNSON, T.J., (1982 'The State and the Professions: Peculiarities of the British', *in* GIDDENS, A. & MacKENZIE, G., (eds.), *Social Class and the Division of Labour*, Cambridge, Cambridge University Press.
KEEBLE, L., (1969), *Principles and Practice of Town and Country Planning*, (Fourth Edition), London, The Estates Gazette.
KIRK, G., (1980), *Urban Planning in a Capitalist Society*, London, Croom Helm.
KLOSTERMAN, R.E., (1985), 'Arguments for and against planning', *Town Planning Review*, vol.56, no.1.
KNOX, P. & CULLEN, J., (1981), 'Planners as urban managers: an exploration of the attitudes and self-image of senior British Planners', *Environment and Planning A*, vol.13, pp.885-989.
KNOX, P., (ed.), (1988), *The Design Professions and the Built Environment*, London, Croom Helm.
LAFFIN, M., (1986), *Professionalism and Policy: The Role of the Professions in the Central-Local Government Relationship*, Aldershot, Gower.
LAFFIN, M. & YOUNG, K., (1990), *Professionalism in Local Government*, Harlow, Longman.

LANE, R.E., (1966), 'The Decline of Politics and Ideology in a Knowledgeable Society', *American Sociological Review*, vol.31, no.5.
LARSON, M.S., (1977), *The Rise of Professionalism: A Sociological Analysis*, California, University of California Press.
LASH, S. & URRY, J., (1988), *The End of Organised Capitalism*, Cambridge, Polity Press.
LIPSKY, M., (1980), *Street-level Bureaucracy*, New York, Russell Sage.
LOW, N.P., (1990), *Planning, Politics and the State: political foundations of planning thought*, London, Unwin Hyman.
MACH, B.W. & WLODZIMIERZ, W., (1986), *Social Mobility and Social Structure*, London, Routledge and Kegan Paul.
MARCUS, S., (1971), 'Planners - Who Are You?', *Journal of the Royal Town Planning Institute*, vol.57, pp.54-59.
MARSDEN, T., LOWE, P. & WHATMORE, S., (1990), *Rural Restructuring: Global Processes and Responses: Critical Perspectives on Rural Change*, vol.1, London, Fulton.
MARSHALL, G., ROSE, D., NEWBY, H. & VOGLER, C., (1989), *Social Class in Modern Britain*, London, Unwin Hyman.
MARSHALL, G., (1990), *In Praise of Sociology*, London, Unwin Hyman.
MARSHALL, G., (1991), 'In defence of class analysis: a comment on R.E. Pahl', *International Journal of Urban and Regional Research*, vol.15, pp.114-18.
McDOUGALL, G., (1979), 'The State, Capital and Land: The History of Town Planning Revisited', *International Journal of Urban and Regional Research*, vol.3, pp.361-380.
McKAY, D.H. & COX, A.W., (1979), *The Politics of Urban Change*, London, Croom Helm.
McLOUGHLIN, J.B., (1969), *Urban and Regional Planning: A Systems Approach*, London, Faber.
McLOUGHLIN, B., (1973), 'The Future of the Planning Profession', *in* COWAN, P., 1973.
MELLOR, J.R., (1977), *Urban Sociology in an Urbanised Society*, London, Routledge and Kegan Paul.
MERTON, R.K., (1982), 'Institutionalised Altruism; The Case of the Professions', *in* MERTON, R.K., *Social Research and the Practicing Professions*, Cambridge (Massachusetts), Arb Books.
MILLERSON, G., (1964), *The Qualifying Associations: A Study in Professionalisation*, London, Routledge and Kegan Paul.
MONTGOMERY, J. & THORNLEY, A., (eds.), (1990), *Radical Planning Initiatives: New Directions for Urban Planning in the 1990s*, Aldershot, Gower.

MOUZELIS, N.P., (1975), *Organisation and Bureaucracy: An analysis of modern theories*, London, Routledge and Kegan Paul.
NADIN, V. & JONES, S., (1990), 'A Profile of the Profession', *The Planner*, January 26.
NORMAN, P., (1975), 'Managerialism: a review of recent work', *in* HARLOE, M., (ed.), *Proceedings of the Conference on Urban Change and Conflict*, London, Centre for Environmental Studies.
NUFFIELD FOUNDATION, (1986), *Town and Country Planning: The Report of a Committee of Inquiry*, London, Nuffield Foundation.
OUCHI, W.G., (1979), 'A Conceptual Framework for the Design of Organisational Control Mechanisms', *Management Science*, 25.
OUCHI, W.G., (1981), *Theory Z: How American Business can meet the Japanese Challenge*, Reading (Mass), Addison-Wesley.
PAGE, E.C., (1985), *Political Authority and Bureaucratic Power*, Hemel Hempstead, Harvester Wheatsheaf.
PAHL, R.E., (1975), *Whose City?*, (second edition), Harmondsworth, Penguin.
PAHL, R.E., (1989), 'Is the emperor naked? Some questions on the adequacy of sociological theory in urban and regional research', *International Journal of Urban and Regional Research*, vol.13, pp.709-20.
PARKIN, F., (1974), *Class Inequlity and Political Order*, New York Praeger.
PARKIN, F., (1979), *Marxism and Class Theory: a Bourgeois Critique*, London, Tavistock.
PARSONS, T., (1949), *The Structure of Social Action*, Illinois, Glencoe Free Press.
PERKIN, H., (1989), *The Rise of Professional Society*, London, Routledge.
PORTER, J., (1965), *The Vertical Mosaic*, Toronto, University of Toronto.
POULANTZAS, N., (1978), *Classes in Contemporary Capitalism*, London, Verso.
POULTON, M. & BEGG, H.M., (1988), 'Public Choice and a Positive Theory of Planning', *The Planner*, pp.15-17, July.
PRANDY, K., (1965), *Professional Employees: A Study of Scientists and Engineers*, London, Faber and Faber.
PRANDY, K., STEWART, A. & BLACKBURN, R.M., *White Collar Work*, London, MacMillan.
PRESSMAN, J. & WILDAVSKY, A., (1973), *Implementation*, Berkeley, University of California Press.
PROTTAS, J.M., (1978), 'The Power of the Street-level Bureaucrat in Public Service Bureaucracies', *Urban Affairs Quarterly*, vol.13(3).
PROTTAS, J.M., (1979), *People Processing: The Street-level Bureaucrat in Public Service Bureaucracies*, Lexington (Massachusetts), D C Heath.

RATTANSI, A., (1985), 'End of an Orthodoxy? The critique of sociology's view of Marx on class', *Sociological Review*, vol.33, no.4, pp.249-52.

RAVETZ, A., (1980), *Remaking Cities: Contradictions of the Recent Urban Environment*, London, Croom Helm.

RAVETZ, A., (1986), *The Government of Space: Town Planning in Modern Society*, London, Faber and Faber.

READE, E., (1987), *British Town and Country Planning*, Milton Keynes, Open University Press.

REISSMAN, L., (1964), *The Urban Process*, New York, Free Press.

RENNER, K., (1953), 'The Service Class', *in* BOTTOMORE, T. & GOODE, P., (eds.), *Austro-Marxism*, Oxford, Clarendon Press.

REX, J. & MOORE, R., (1967), *Race, Community and Conflict*, Oxford, Oxford University Press.

ROBERTS, M., (1991), *Living in a Man-made World: Gender Assumptions in Modern Housing Design*, London, Routledge.

ROEMER, J., (1982), *A General Theory of Exploitation and Class*, Cambridge (Massachusetts), Harvard University Press.

ROSE, D., (1988), *Social Stratification and Economic Change*, London, Hutchinson.

ROYAL TOWN PLANNING INSTITUTE, (1976), *Planning and the Future*, London, RTPI.

ROYAL TOWN PLANNING INSTITUTE/COMMISSION FOR RACIAL EQUALITY, (1983), *Planning for a Multi-racial Britain*, London, CRE.

ROYAL TOWN PLANNING INSTITUTE, (1990), *Directory of Planning Consultants*, London, RTPI.

RUESCHEMEYER, D., (1983), 'Professional Autonomy and the Social Control of Expertise', *in* DINGWALL, R. & LEWIS, P., 1983.

SAUNDERS, P., (1990), *A Nation of Home Owners*, London, Unwin Hyman.

SARRE, P., (1989), 'Recomposition of the Class Structure', *in* HAMNETT, C., McDOWELL, L. & SARRE, P., (eds.), *The Changing Social Structure*, London, Sage.

SALAMAN, G., (1979), *Work Organisations: Resistance and Control*, London, Longman.

SAVAGE, M., (1987), *Spatial Mobility and the Professional Labour Market, Urban and Regional Studies Working Paper No 56*, Brighton, University of Sussex.

SAVAGE, M., DICKENS, P. & FIELDING, T., (1988), 'Some Social and Political Implications of the Contemporary Fragmentation of the 'Service Class' in Britain', *International Journal of Urban and Regional Research*, pp.455-76.

SAVAGE, M. & FIELDING, A., (1989), *Class Formation and Regional Development: The 'Service Class' in South-East England*, Geoforum 20(2): 203-18.

SAVAGE, M., (1989), *The Structure of the 'Middle Class' in a Growth Area: the case of Berkshire*, University of Sussex.

SAVAGE, M., BARLOW, J., DICKENS, P. & FIELDING, A., (1992), *Property, Bureaucracy and Culture: Middle Class Formation in Contemporary Britain*, London, Routledge.

SCASE, R., (1977), *Industrial Society - Class, Cleavage and Control*, New York, St Martin's Press.

SCASE, R. & GOFFEE, R., (1982), *The Entrepreneurial Middle Class*, London, Croom Helm.

'SCHUSTER', (1950), *Report of the Committee on the Qualifications of Planners*, Ministry of Town and Country Planning, London, HMSO.

SCHMITTER, P.C., (1974), 'Still the Century of Corporation?', *Review of Politics 36*, pp.85-131.

'SCOTT', (1943), *Report of the Committee on Land Utilisation in Rural Areas*, London, HMSO.

SCOTT, J., (1982), *The Upper Classes*, London, MacMillan.

SCOTT, W.R., (1966), 'Professionals in Bureaucracies' *in* VOLLMER, H. & MILLS, D.M., 1966.

SHORT, J., FLEMING, S., & WITT, S., (1986), *Housebuilding, Planning and Community Action*, London, Runtlidge and Kegan Paul.

SHEPLEY, C., & FRYER, D., (1991), '1991, 1992 ... What Every Planner needs to know about Europe', *The Planner*, 15.2.91.

SIMMIE, J., (1974), *Citizens in Conflict*, London, Hutchinson.

SIMMIE, J., (1987), *Power, Property and Corporatism: the Political Sociology of Planning*, London, MacMillan.

SIMMIE, J. & FRENCH, S., (1989), *Corporatism, Participation and Planning: the Case of London*, Oxford, Pergammon.

SMITH, B.C., (1988), *Bureaucracy and Political Power*, Brighton, Wheatsheaf.

SOHN-RETHEL, A., (1978), *Intellectual and Manual Labour*, London, MacMillan.

STEWART, A., PRANDY, K. & BLACKBURN, R., (1980), *Social Stratification and Occupations*, London, MacMillan.

STREEK, W. & SCHMITTER, P.C., (eds.), (1985), *Private Interest Government: beyond market and state*, London, Sage.

THOMPSON, E.P., (1965), 'Peculiarities of the English', *in* MILIBAND, R. & SAVILLE, J., *The Social Register*, London, Merlin Press.

THOMPSON, R., (1990), *Believing in Planning*, The Planner, January, 1990.

THORNLEY, A., (1988a), *Planning and the Ideology of the New Right*, Paper for the Second Annual AESOP Conference, Dortmund, November.

THORNLEY, A., (1988b), 'Planning in a Cool Climate: The Effects of Thatcherism', *The Planner*, pp.17-19.

THORNLEY, A., (1991), *Urban Planning under Thatcherism: The Challenge of the Market*, London, Routledge.

UNDERWOOD, J., (1980), *Town Planners in Search of a Role*, SAUS Occasional Paper, no.6, Bristol, School for Advanced Urban Studies.

UNDERWOOD, J., (1987), 'Development Control: A Case Study of Discretion in Action', *in* BARRETT, S., & FUDGE, C., 1981.

URRY, J., (1981), *The Anatomy of Capitalist Societies*, London, MacMillan.

'UTTHWATT', (1942), *Final Report of the Expert Committee on Compensation and Betterment*, London, HMSO.

VOLLMER, H.M. & MILLS, D.M., (eds.), (1966), *Professionalisation*, New Jersey, Prentice Hall.

WALBY, S., (1986), *Patriarchy at Work*, Cambridge, Polity.

WALKER, P., (1979), *Between Capital and Labour*, New York, Monthly Review.

WALTERS, P., (1975), *'Professionalisation and the Routinisation of Charisma in Town Planning'*, Paper delivered to the History of Planning Group, Birmingham, March 15.

WEBER, M., (1968), *Economy and Society*, ROTH, G., (ed.), New York, Bedminster Press.

WILDING, P., (1982), *Professional Power and Social Welfare*, London, Routledge and Kegan Paul.

WILLIAMS, P., (1978), 'Urban Managerialism: A Concept of Relevance?', *Area 10*, pp.236-240.

WILLIAMSON, P.J., (1989), *Corporatism in Perspective: An Introductory Guide to Corporatist Theory*, London, Sage.

WILLMOTT, P., (1986), *Social Networks, Informal Care and Public Policy*, London, Policy Study Institute.

WILSON, E., (1977), *Women and the Welfare State*, London, Tavistock.

WRIGHT, E.O., (1979), *Class, Crisis and the State*, London, Verso.

WRIGHT, E.O., (1985), *Classes*, New York, Verso.

WRIGHT, E.O., (ed.), (1989), *The Debate on Classes*, New York, Verso.